HAND TO

HAND TO MOUTH

Hand to Mouth
The teething troubles of business and babies

Jodine O'Donoghue Boothby

HAND TO MOUTH

Text Copyright © Jodine O'Donoghue Boothby 2017

Jodine O'Donoghue Boothby has asserted her right in accordance with the Copyright Designs and Patents Act 1988 to be identified as the author of this work.

All rights reserved

No part of this publication may be lent, resold, hired out or reproduced in any form or by any means without prior written permission from the author and publisher. All rights reserved.
Copyright © 3P Publishing

First published in 2017 in the UK

3P Publishing
C E C, London Road
Corby
NN17 5EU

A catalogue number for this book is available from the British Library

ISBN 978-1-911559-42-9

HAND TO MOUTH

For Jimmy and Charlie,
my little hand chewing, early teething babies!

HAND TO MOUTH

HAND TO MOUTH

Contents:
Preface	1
Acknowledgements	5
Foreword by Theo Paphitis	7
Chapter 1. Confidence, Maths …..	9
Chapter 2. Pasties, Parties and Boobs	24
Chapter 3. Depression, eBay and BOB	34
Chapter 4. Babies, socks and GERD	45
Chapter 5. A light bulb, Sophie, ….	51
Chapter 6: For the love of gLOVE	69
Chapter 7: Barb wire clad Porcupine's, ….	88
Chapter 8: Dragons, Angels …..	101
Chapter 9: Psychiatric help,	114
Chapter 10: Police checks,…	121
Chapter 11: See-through dresses,	137
Chapter 12: China, Germany, USA	150
Chapter 13: Taming a dragon, stalking ….	160
Chapter 14: Plastic willy's, Fibromyalgia	171
Chapter 15: Big retailers, hippy's, …..	183
Chapter 16: Hohoho, #gummeeteatime ….	190

HAND TO MOUTH

HAND TO MOUTH

Preface:

I decided to write this book because I have always wanted to write a book, however, I never really knew what to write about. I have always worn my heart on my sleeve, and up until recently, I was never very emotionally intelligent. I have also always kept a diary, which was the traditional style diary up until 2007, and then Facebook became my new format. I believe there are two main reasons for wanting to keep a diary. There is the diary that you keep hidden, and very safe because there are secrets and things in there that even *you* can't bear to read. And then there is wanting to write because your brain simply needs to process events, thoughts or feelings, and make sense of them. Mine is the latter.

The Gummee story has been an exciting, emotional, exhausting, exhilarating journey and I wanted to share how the world's first teething mitten (designed solely for babies to wear), was launched. I also wanted to humanise my brand, demonstrating the passion and care behind the brand, our products, and business as a whole. Over the last ten years, I have come to love business in general, not just my own, and in writing this book, I hope that my story inspires other budding entrepreneurs.

This book is a little bit about me, and the events that lead up to the invention and subsequent launch of the Gummee glove, our flagship product, and in turn the founding of my now successful, international brand of baby products. It is about a young lady who flitted from job to job, and place to place, like a gnat with restless wing syndrome. It is about actual, real-life angels, and wanting copycats to birth barb-wire clad porcupines. It is about unbelievable success and near-soul destroying failures. It is about lockjaw inducing determination and tenacity, and unfaltering defiance in the face of IBS inducing obstacles. It's about feeling the fear, and taking the bull by both of its horns, and ramming its head up its own damn backside. It's about the fact that you can achieve the most amazing things, with passion, bravery, tenacity, dedication, and a whole lot of gLOVE.

I hope that this book helps to inspire and encourage anyone who has that entrepreneurial streak but may be convinced that they don't have the funds, courage, knowledge, qualifications or resources to take their idea anywhere.

HAND TO MOUTH

Writing this book has been an amazing experience. I have gained real insight into the person that I am, and I have wanted to shake myself silly as much as I have wanted to hug myself. I have been forced to look at my total lack of emotional control at times, and I have cringed and scalded myself. I have written about certain events and thought countless times, 'if only I knew then, what I now know....' hindsight is a wonderful thing, and writing this book has shown me that, quite a lot.

There were particularly difficult times in my life that I started to write about, and I had to stop writing for a few days, or even weeks. I have revisited some really painful events in my life, and they served as wonderful reminders of just how lucky I am, and how wonderful my life is now.

I have seen, and understood, that my brain is controlled by two different Jodine's. The emotional one needs to take a back seat, at the right times. The Jodine that deals with facts, and calm, and common sense, and control - she's fucking awesome and I want to be her all the time. But emotional Jodine quite often gags and bounds sensible Jodine, causes painful fingers with fury typing, creates clothes tightening through endless devouring of luxury ice cream, Lindt chocolate, and pickled onion Monster Munch sandwiches,

HAND TO MOUTH

and says and does stupid things that can't be taken back. You will notice that emotional Jodine has taken over writing in this book at various points. Those points are usually noticeable, with lots of words written in italic, because she likes to emphasise her points, and really convey her emotion.

Writing this book has allowed me to reach through the shit storms of my mind, grab sensible, calm Jodine by the hand, and lead her to the front. She is currently going through training and preparing to take over emotional Jodine, in her new role as brain director.

I feel like this book has helped me to rescue myself.

HAND TO MOUTH

Acknowledgements:

Stephen. My husband. Beneath the rugged (in a homeless, smelly kind of a way) good looks, is a heart of gold, and it belongs to me. You make me feel like the luckiest woman on the planet, every single day, and without you, my life would not be *this* life. Everything that we are, and everything that we have, has been co-created with you, my soul mate and best friend.

Thank you for being my solid base, my constant, and for not telling me off for my double standards when it comes to farting.

Thank you for pulling my stupid ass back down out of the clouds whenever I need it, and doing it with love and patience.

Thank you to everyone that is mentioned in this book; even the ones I have used pseudonyms for. Without all of you, there would be no story.

Thanks to Andy, at 3P Publishing, for your suggestion for the title of this book, it is perfect. (Not the book, the title. I'll let you, dear reader, decide what the book is like.)

HAND TO MOUTH

Lucy, Kate, Sam, Sally-Anne, Jessica, Alan and Trevor. Thanks will never be enough, but you know I love, and appreciate, all that you do for Gummee.

Read on, dear reader. It's going to be a bumpy read.

HAND TO MOUTH

Foreword by Theo Paphitis, Retail Entrepreneur

To succeed in business, you have to learn from your mistakes as it is very, very rare to get it right first time. If successful people fall down, they will get right back up again, dust themselves off and learn from their mistakes. They may fall over numerous times, but as long as they're learning and adapting how they do things, they're onto a winner.

No one successful ever gave up the first time or accepted 'no' for an answer. They created, pushed, changed and made sure that they had every base covered through research and as I like to call it, doing their homework. That is business in a nutshell for me. Know your market, research the hell out of it, and keep up your momentum. People who do this will succeed…and Jodine is one of those people.

Jodine is one of my #SBS (Small Business Sunday) winners and the fact that she entered several times before winning is an absolute testament to the fact that she is a tenacious character who doesn't give up easily in her pursuit to succeed. Jodine spoke in front of almost 1000 #SBS businesses in February 2017 at our annual event, and her candid story resonated with so many of them who have also built up businesses over the years from nothing or are aspiring to.

If you like your entrepreneurs polished and pretentious then this book isn't for you, but if you want them real, honest and passionate then get the kettle on, put your feet up and read about her rollercoaster of a journey in building her business Gummee from scratch.

Theo Paphitis, entrepreneur

HAND TO MOUTH

Chapter 1. Confidence, Maths, and Dinosaur rubbers.

I did not learn very well at school. I was not academic, and I did not learn well in a classroom environment. I had no confidence whatsoever. Don't get me wrong; it wasn't that I didn't want to learn, I really *did* want to learn! I wanted to make my parents proud. I would go into a classroom, full of enthusiasm, start a fresh new page, start listening to the teacher…….and then I'd be off into my own little dream world. Drifting from wondering what it would be like to be the most beautiful girl in the classroom, or the cleverest, or funniest…….to suddenly back in the room thinking: 'Shit, what did I miss? What did Sir just say?' Everyone would be scribbling away in their books, and I'd be too scared to put my hand up and say: 'Sorry Sir, I was daydreaming, could you please repeat what you just said?'

I'd try to retain the information that I learned, I would take it in *while* it was being explained, but ask me to repeat it five minutes later. I'm sorry, my brain only understood and took it in *while* you were explaining it. I didn't *memorise* it, silly! I would understand bits of what was being taught, but being too afraid to put up my hand when there were bits that I did not understand? I did not have the confidence to do that. Speak up, in front of a class full of students, admitting I didn't understand? No way. I didn't want the attention on me. So, knowing I did not fully understand a topic or subject, I think internally, I'd already resigned myself to failure most of the time.

I attended Cardinal Newman Roman Catholic secondary School in Keresley, Coventry. I'd been moved there in my second year of secondary school due to going through a bit of bullying, so I was already a scared little mouse. It is safe to say that I did not like school.

I think hate is probably a little too strong a word, but my memory of school is not one of fondness. I couldn't wait to leave. I had a small circle of really good friends, and my time spent with them was fun, and memorable, for all the right reasons. I am still good friends with them now, and when we're together, we truly go back to our youth for the time that we're together.

Needless to say, I left school with no qualifications and got into the sixth form by the skin of my teeth. I still remember the look of disappointment on Dad's face when I climbed into the van with my GCSE certificates after I'd collected them from school. 2 D's, 2 E's and the rest were F's. Apart from two U's, which stood for 'unmarked'. My Dad is my king. There is no one like him. Apart from my brother Pete (you know its true, Pete). My Dad was very strict. I say *was* because he is less strict with the grandkids. (You've chilled out a lot, Dad.) To disappoint him, was to fail in life. I have always had a huge amount of respect for him, and nothing scared me more than letting him down.

He also has the most unbelievable imagination and used to dream up the most hilarious ways to entertain us as kids. One of my favourite memories was going out for a walk to 'the money tree's' at the Slough, in Coventry. We obviously didn't realise it at the time, but he'd wear trousers that had holes in the pockets and fill them with coins. He'd walk on in front, weaving in and out of the trees, calling back to us to walk slowly, in case we missed any of the coins. He'd be dropping them on to the ground through his pockets, and me and Teresa would be transfixed. Not daring to move our eyes off the ground while we followed along behind Dad, not wanting to miss any coins. I wonder why I never looked up to see if there were coins on the branches? Pete on the other hand would be running off ahead of my

HAND TO MOUTH

Dad, determined to be the first to spot the coins and, therefore, collect the most money.

He never found any by using that method though. I still piss myself laughing, remembering back to him screaming his head off because he couldn't find any.

I digress! Back to my lack of education. I had no qualifications to get into the sixth form with but somehow was still able to stay on to do a basic business course. I think I just thought it would be a bit of a doss at the time. However, I also thought it sounded impressive, and I liked being able to tell people: "Oh, I'm studying business".

Maths was my absolute *worst* subject at school. I *hated* it. The clearest picture I have, of any of my teachers, is my maths teacher. Her look of disdain, at yet another failed attempt on my part, to understand yet another mathematical problem that I am sure would have been useful at some point in my life up to now. (Nope. And as adults, we are allowed to use calculators, wherever and whenever we like. We have calculators on our phones.)

I failed Foundation Business studies. I think I spent most of the time hiding in bushes outside the school gates, smoking. Sorry Mum, sorry

HAND TO MOUTH

Dad. I then applied for college, resolving to change, and do it properly. Leisure and tourism. I could *so* be an air hostess! That seemed like a fun, glamorous job! I quickly discovered I was never going to be tall enough to be an air hostess. So again, my eagerness to learn and do something with my life other than drift along, soon waned and I was back to the internal voice; reminding me that I was not destined for anything great. My old Maths teachers voice repeating: 'You'll never amount to anything!! Are you stupid?" in my head. And my inner voice replying: 'I think so.'

I'd had paid jobs up until this point. I'd worked as a Saturday girl at my Auntie Sarah's hairdressing salon where my Mum also worked. I say Auntie; she is my Mum's best friend but is more like an Auntie to me and my siblings. I'd also worked part-time at a newsagents in Coventry City centre. I packed magazines at various warehouses around Coventry, I did strawberry picking, call centre work, I was a chambermaid, and the list goes on.

I think I must have been mentally lazy, but I always worked. Money and independence motivated me. At the age of fifteen, my parents went through a very bitter divorce. My world as I knew it, came crashing down. As well as disliking school, home life was quite unstable during and after my parent's divorce. We moved to a different area of Coventry with my Mum, while Dad stayed in the family home. Dad was absolutely heart-broken, a totally broken man. Which in turn, broke my heart, too.

I have two brothers and a sister. My older brother, Brendan, spent a lot of time raving, being out with his friends, and spending time at Her Majesty's Pleasure, so he missed quite a bit of what was going on.

My younger brother, Peter, is only eleven months younger than me, and my little sister Teresa, is three-and-a-half years younger. I can only speak for how I felt throughout the divorce, of course, but I am sure we were all affected somehow or other. I was and have always been very close to my siblings and my parents. I was best friends with my Mum throughout my late teen years and spent most weekends out with her and Auntie Sarah. I went out almost every Friday, Saturday and Sunday night from the age of sixteen to nineteen, and I especially enjoyed Sunday nights out with my Mum. We'd often be staggering through Coventry city centre, from pub to pub; laughing so much we cried, and/or pee'd a bit, hence the staggering.

HAND TO MOUTH

I had some fights with my younger brother Pete, but most of the time we got on pretty well and hung around with the same group of friends. His best friend was David, or Speedy, as he was known back then, and I fancied him rotten. However, I wasn't a particularly fanciable teenager, and whenever I had a crush on one of my brother's friends, they nearly always fancied my best mate instead. That was usually my cousin, Claire or another of my friends. I always felt like the ugly one, lurking in the shadows of the gorgeous one. I was the one passing love notes between the gorgeous girl and the fit lad that I fancied. You know, before text messages and stuff. David did agree to go out with me once, but then kissed me and said my breath stank. And, consequently, dumped me. Great. I was now the ugly one with bad breath. Until I started going out with my first serious boyfriend, I resigned myself to the role of tomboy and daredevil. As if carrying out the dares that no one else had the bottle to do would impress the boys. Some sort of weird compensation for being too ugly to date? If only I could visit my past self.

Not long after my parents split up, my Dad started a new relationship. My Mum could not handle this, so it was then her turn to have the breakdown. I remember her being in bed and very sad, quite a lot of the time. I remember heartbreaking moments of her begging my Dad to come and visit us late at night because she wanted him back. He would come, but only because he was worried about her, and us, and how she was coping.

One night, he stood in the porch of Mum's place, and hugged me and Teresa, while we sobbed, not knowing how to help them. He told me that I smelled like my Mum. It is funny how a tiny little insignificant comment, can affect you in devastating ways. When they were going through a really bad patch of detesting each other, they would each say mean things about the other. Because he'd said some mean things about my Mum, I somehow believed that he didn't like me, because I reminded him of my Mum. It took years for me to explain to him how I'd felt, and he was clearly shocked. I always knew deep down that he didn't dislike me, but when you're a teenager going through something so devastating, it doesn't occur to you that your feelings about something should be heard or considered, they had enough to deal with already.

Dad had no interest in getting back together with my Mum; it was too late for that. I felt absolutely devastated and made it my life mission to get them back together. But alas, it was not meant to be. It felt like the solid family unit that we always were, and had always been, was rocked to its absolute core, and then split completely in two.

My boyfriend became my escapism. He was a loveable lad, a rogue, some might say. I had fallen in love with him at the age of nine. My nine-year-old self would glare at you very defiantly right now if you were to *dare* say that you cannot fall in love at such a young age. She would wake you up every night, to show you her tears, and ask you why he is all she can think about, day and night? She would tell you how she stood looking out of the family bathroom window one night, gazing at the night sky, tears rolling down her cheeks when she saw a shooting star. She wished upon that shooting star, that one day Colin (not his real name) would finally see that they should be together.

The day before this night, a school day, Colin had waited for the teacher to leave the room at reading time. He then sat next to her at her table. In front of a room full of silent children, he asked her if he could have one of her rubbers. (I had an amazing collection of pencil erasers.) I was thrilled that he was sitting next to me, and talking to me, let alone anything else. He said: 'If I go out with you, will you give me one of your rubbers?' I gave him two. They were Dinosaur rubbers, with wobbling eyes. My prized rubbers. He went back to his desk, sat down, and called over: 'Thanks. You're chucked!' I was heartbroken and mortified. Hence, the heartbreak and the wish upon a shooting star.

At age fourteen, I'd gone through the bullying at the local secondary school, which is also where Colin went. He had tried to help me once, on a particularly bad day when he'd found me crying on a bench in the school. I still saw him every now and then, in the local area, just to say 'hi' or wave to.

Not very long before my parents split up for good, I was attending a local dance school. It was just something I did for fun, with a couple of close friends. I had no rhythm at all, so I didn't take it seriously. Thank god camera phones didn't exist back then. We used to walk to dance class, a mile up the main road from my house, at a local sports centre. On the way back home one night, we passed Colin and a load of his friends, all taking shelter in the doorway of a block of flats. We all awkwardly shouted 'hello' and carried on walking. I got home, and a little while later the doorbell rang. It was one of my best friends at the time, Louise. "Colin has just asked me to knock your door. He says he wants to go out with either you or me. Are you interested?"

HAND TO MOUTH

I was elated. Not because he had asked Louise to knock my door and ask me out (Ok, ok! Giving me the option of him being allowed to choose between me and Louise! - who by the way, would have given Barbie a run for her money, with her beautiful big, long, bouncing, naturally curly and blonde hair and the shapeliest legs and figure you've ever seen), but because I could finally get my own back for the time that he stole my rubbers and chucked me in front of the whole class!

"Tell him (I said) - that he doesn't have a choice. Tell him to go out with you!"

Louise giggled, and off she went. I can't tell you how that moment made me feel. How empowering! I still fancied the living shit out of this guy, and instead of falling to pieces like a flattered little girl, instead of turning into a romanticised zombie, *I turned him down.*

A little while later, the doorbell rang again. It was Louise.
"He said he doesn't want to go out with me now. He wants to go out with you."
I laughed. "Tell him to meet me, 7pm tomorrow night, outside Steve's shop."

HAND TO MOUTH

Steve's shop was a local off-license we'd hang around inside or outside, depending on when Steve had had enough, and he'd serve us alcohol, as well as sell us single cigarettes for thirteen pence each. Oh, the 90's.

So Colin and I became a couple. It was the typical tale of two sweethearts. He'd always be late, turn up stoned out of his box and I'd dump him, over and over again. I was constantly arguing with him about cannabis - or draw, as we called it. I wanted him to stop smoking it; he didn't want to. In the end, and with Mum and Dad too busy going through a bitter break up to really notice, I started smoking cannabis, too. I told myself 'If you can't beat 'em, join 'em!' (I don't smoke it anymore. I gave up in September 2003.)

I don't want anyone to think badly of my parents, and I don't want anyone to think that I think badly of my parents, or that I judge them for how they handled the divorce.

Experiences are how we learn. I don't judge my parents for how they handled their break up; I only remember the pain we all felt at the time. I learned a lot about how I would handle a break up if I were ever to find myself in a similar situation if kids were involved. Looking back, I appreciate just how hard it must have been for both of them. My Dad had the whole rejection to deal with and the splitting up of the family unit, and my Mum went from thinking she didn't love my Dad, to realising that she couldn't be without him, but it was too late. There is nothing worse than seeing your parents go through absolute heartbreak and being completely helpless to do anything about it.

I moved out with my Mum to the new home; then I moved back to the old family home, which was now Dad's. I moved back with Mum to yet another new home, and then moved back to my Dad's again when I started college.

Before the old family home, we'd lived in Wales for four years. When we moved to Wales, I was five, and I had to go to a Welsh language school for a year to learn Welsh so that I could then attend the local school. Our first home in Wales was amazing. It sat right at the top of a hill in a beautiful village called Nefyn. The beach was just over the road. The garden was huge, with an eight-berth caravan on one side. I remember that caravan so well; 'cooking' in there with my siblings. We made 'butter pop', which was basically heated up orange juice with knobs of butter thrown in. Absolutely gross. And bloody dangerous. I remember Mum and Dad inviting a family to come and stay in the caravan; they knew the

HAND TO MOUTH

family from Coventry. One afternoon, we all sat in the living room and the guy that my Dad knew, the father from the guest family, said how wonderful the caravan was and how much they were enjoying their stay. I felt it was a great moment to interrupt, and proudly declare how my Dad had sourced everything in the caravan, even down to the cutlery, from the local tip. I'll never forget the way my Dad glared at me.

My maternal Grandad and uncle and aunt and cousins lived fairly close to us in Wales, but still a long drive away. It was a fairly scary, unsettling time, and even at that young age I knew and felt that we didn't quite 'fit in' with the locals, or at the school, even though I could speak fluent Welsh by the time I started there. We moved after a couple of years, to somewhere else in Wales and yet another school. It's no wonder really that I have always struggled to settle, and then actually feel settled. So, the old family home in Coventry was actually our fifth home.

I have moved another ten times since then.

I moved out to live with Colin at the age of eighteen, into a pokey little flat that was mainly used as a place for him and his friends to get stoned and drunk, while I worked. Colin had odd jobs and worked on and off for a car wash company, as well as lots of unknown dodgy dealings. I once came home from work to find our bedroom full of computers. The news in the *Coventry Evening Telegraph* that evening was about the local college being broken into, and computers were stolen. Within a couple of weeks of that happening and me threatening to leave if they didn't get rid of the computers, I came home to find Colin passed out on the toilet. Pants around his ankles, crushed drinks can at his feet, a spoon, some tin foil and other bits such as rolling paper, a lighter and whatever else had fallen out of his pockets while he was in his oblivious, drug-addled state. I write about this with sympathy for him, and also the anger I felt at the time, towards him, for doing this to himself. I packed my things into a few bin liners that day and marched over to my Dads. Colin and I never really had any closure. I just told him I was leaving, and he was so out of his face, he didn't even bother to argue. He probably didn't even realise I was even there that afternoon. That was the last time I saw him.

HAND TO MOUTH

Chapter 2. Pasties, Parties and Boobs.

Within a couple of weeks, I'd arranged to go to Cornwall for a two-week holiday. My best friend in the whole world since birth, who also happens to be my cousin, Claire, had moved to Cornwall when we were fifteen. I felt like my right arm had been torn off. I missed her so much, especially with everything that was going on. I literally pined for her. I was over the moon to be heading off to Cornwall with her. She'd been to Coventry to visit some of her family on her mother's side. Her mum is my Auntie Pauline, and she had been married to my Dad's brother, who had moved to Spain long ago.

Claire was very excited as we were to be travelling in her new car. I can only remember that it was a red car, I don't remember the make of it. She could not legally drive as she was taking her driving lessons at the time, so the car was being driven by a friend of Auntie Pauline's partner. We loaded up the car with my suitcases, and I was beside myself with excitement. I couldn't wait to start my new single life with a full two weeks of non-stop partying!

HAND TO MOUTH

Just outside of Coventry, on a motorway, we were pulled over by a police car. The driver of our car was taken to the police car behind us to be questioned, while an officer sat in the car with myself and Claire and just made small talk. It turned out that the driver of the car had several warrants out for his arrest, so he had to remain in custody. The officer in our car drove us to the nearest services, and from there Claire and I were supposed to contact whoever we could to come and pick us up. When we pulled into the services, there were a few more police cars, waiting for us. We had to remain in the car while it was searched.

A plastic bag was found in the back of the car, which contained a large amount of cannabis. Apparently, it was quite a lot. Not the sort of amount that warranted a little warning and a slap on the wrist. It was the sort of amount that would result in a lengthy custodial sentence. It was an absolutely terrifying day. Claire and I were taken into police custody and separated into cells. I think we spent two nights there, possibly one, but it felt like an eternity. Detailed memory of it is sort of fuzzy. It really was one of the scariest things I have ever been through.

The police were actually very kind and took good care of us. Once we'd both been interviewed, we were put in a cell together. When Claire first came into my cell, we just held each other and sobbed. After a while, whilst mumbling to each other about how scared we were and how sorry she was that it had been her car, I made a comment about how the police station food was shit, and that their so-called fish fingers had caused my plastic fork to break. We burst out laughing, and then we were crying with laughter. I don't think we stopped laughing. We did handstands and complained to each other about the disgusting little piss tin in the corner of the cell. The police obviously knew that the find was nothing to do with us and that we were innocent. However, they were not prepared to let us go until someone admitted to the ownership of the crime. They even popped over to the local Spar and bought us fags and bottles of coke.

The person responsible handed himself in, and we were free to leave.

I couldn't continue with my plans to holiday in Cornwall and instead had to return to Coventry to sign on at the local police station every single day at three o'clock until the case was dealt with. This meant that I couldn't work full time, so I took part-time work in the evenings through an agency, at a cheque encoding centre for HSBC. After three months, the court agreed that mine and Claire's records were to be wiped clean. We no longer had to sign on at the police station, it was all over, and I was finally free to get my backside to Cornwall for that holiday. I met my next boyfriend, Symon, during the holiday and he came to visit me in Coventry every few weeks after I returned home. I'd landed a job at Barclays telephone banking centre, and my Mum and Dad finally seemed proud of me. I felt proud of me too, but I still hated the job. My confidence was still at an all-time low, despite gaining a certificate of accreditation for over 90% call quality, whatever that meant.

I decided to move to Cornwall. I had visited a few times, missed Claire like crazy, had a new Cornish boyfriend, and I wanted what I thought would just be a year out. Traveling, (okay, travelling to various pubs in Cornwall) and partying, and having adventures (in various pubs in Cornwall). I remember the day I was moving.

My Dad had packed his van with all of my belongings. I was sitting nervously on my bed, tearful after having said goodbye to my Mum, and my best friends the night before. My Dad sat on the end of my bed and said: "Jodine, I will support you. I will take you down there, with all of your things, and you only have to click your fingers if you need me, I will be straight back to get you. But I think you're being a twat, and you're making the biggest mistake of your life."

It was the only time in my life that I remember going completely against my Dad's opinion, and still going ahead with my plans. Looking back, I think it was because he was proud of the fact that I finally had a good job, and because his daughter was moving away and he was going to miss me. In my mind though, it wasn't final. I thought I'd be gone for a few weeks of partying, then I'd be back, like the home bird I really thought I was.

I took up my next job, in yet another role that I hated, at a cafe in Tavistock, Devon. I'd moved into a shared house with Claire, her boyfriend, and another lad called Nathan. We had a lot of fun, partying and just enjoying life.

Six months later, Claire moved to Spain with her boyfriend. (I'm sensing a theme here Claire if you're reading.) I started yet another job at a hotel in Tavistock. My job was to run the bar and take orders for afternoon pastries and cream teas.

One day, a party of around twelve people came in, and they all wanted to be served cream teas. I needed help and went off to find my manager as there was only me on the bar on this particular afternoon. I found him, smoking in the staff room and explained I needed help. He didn't even look in my direction. He exhaled some smoke from his cigarette and just tilted his head to one side, not taking his eyes off the television. I was furious. I went back upstairs to the kitchen, lined up all of the orders on the side, and I collected my bag and my coat, and I left.

Needless to say, I was gutted about Claire going to Spain, but I was well into my new relationship with Symon, and we decided to move in together. This relationship was a very volatile one. We drank too much, partied too much and argued constantly. We were not a good match. The next four years were a bit of a blur, while I worked and partied, fell out with Symon, worked and partied and fell back in with Symon. It was an unhealthy, never-ending cycle.

Towards the end of my first year of moving to Cornwall, and after leaving three more job roles, I got a job on the factory floor at a food manufacturer. I was on a production line full of women, crimping Cornish pasties by hand. It was this job that made me realise why I hated most of the jobs I'd had before. I did not like customer service! Because of my confidence issues, and the fact that I was a total people pleaser, I did not trust myself to give customers the correct information about anything. I couldn't trust my brain

HAND TO MOUTH

to absorb information correctly and *then* regurgitate it correctly to a customer. This was especially true in roles where the information was important, such as telephone banking or customer service at British Telecom.

Up until I started work at Tamarfoods, I'd had twenty-seven different jobs. My job at Tamarfoods was my twenty-eighth. I loved working on the shop floor. It was really hard work at first. I remember telling Symon's Mum, Jayne, that I'd got the job. Before I started, she'd said to me: 'Ooh. That'll 'arden yer' (That was a Cornish accent, by the way, and what she meant was that this job would turn me inside out, make me ache in places I didn't realise it was possible to ache and work me so hard that I wanted to physically throw up at least twice a day, for like, a month.) I had no idea what she meant at the time though.

And then I started. On my first day, I'd worn shoe's that had a heel on them - no one had warned me that I would need comfortable shoes. A twelve-hour shift, of hard laborious work in a factory. Of course, I wasn't going to realise what sort of shoes I needed. Ahem.

On top of the shoes, for hygiene purposes, I had to wear plastic shoe covers. The first job I was given, was to stand at the end of a production line, taking off massive metal trays from under a protracting belt, then load the trays full of pasties into big metal trolley racks that were then wheeled away into an industrial oven. I dropped a lot of trays of pasties onto my feet that day, and I almost asked to go for a pee, and instead walk out the door and not look back. But there was no way that I could afford to do that.

On this same day, a young man, I say young, he was about my age, came up and introduced himself to me. "Hi, my name is Steve, I work on the ovens. If you need anything, just give me a shout. Either me or Kai will be around to give you a hand!"

Steve is now my husband, but we didn't get together until around three years later.

After three years of working on the factory floor, I'd made some awesome friends. I started to get a familiar feeling and knew it was time for something new.

I applied for an internal position, to be a Quality Assurance officer. At the time, I was due to go on sick leave for an operation. I was told I had the job and was absolutely over the moon. I was to leave, have my operation, recover, and then return to work to start my new role. There was a change coming! Mostly in my boobs.

I spent a lot of time at the doctors complaining about my breasts, as they'd never fully developed. I mean, one grew and just about measured a 30aa. The other did not grow, and also had a permanently inverted nipple. For someone who's confidence was already stunted, this was the icing on the cake. My self-esteem loved to batter me senseless with my non-existent breasticles. It was a daily occurrence, in front of the mirror. Ooh, my hair looks good. Loving my ass in these jeans! Oh fuck. The stuffing in my right bra cup is lopsided. How do I secure that, before a long shift at work? What shall I wear when I go out this weekend? As long as it keeps the stuffing in place and reveals no part of my upper body *at all*, I'm sure it'll be fucking fiiiiiine!

My boobs, or lack, there of, sure did give me anger issues. After a long history of complaint to the doctor, the NHS agreed to do something about it. I realised something needed to be done when it suddenly dawned on me that there was absolutely no way in a million years that I was ever going to go swimming or to the beach in a sexy bikini. Yes, yes, I know. Having a great body with perfect boobs is not the be all and end all, I know that *now*. I didn't know it back then. I was insecure, and back then, it was important to me to at least be in proportion. I missed a lot of trips to the beach with my friends.

Something had to be done. Or rather, two things had to be done. Since they couldn't get a breast implant small enough to match my non-existent boob to the other side, I was told to pick a size. I asked the doc to use his best judgement, and just make sure I was in proportion.

When I came around from the operation, one of the first friends I ever made in Cornwall, Lisa, still a very close friend to this day, was sitting by my bed. I remember feeling bitterly disappointed because, for some reason, I thought they'd not gone ahead with the operation. I cried and asked why they hadn't done it yet. Lisa laughed, pulled my top open, and said: 'Look! They're there!!'

My two new little mounds of confidence-restoring glory. I finally felt *normal*. My new found body confidence was a huge help for the new role at work.

Chapter 3. Depression, eBay and BOB

I had ended my relationship with Sy, and within a month I was in another relationship with my now husband, Steve. I'd also started my new role at work, and my life had completely changed. My relationship with Symon could also actually be defined as my party years. And I'd partied *a lot.* Probably a lot harder than I should have. Actually, definitely a lot harder than I should have.

I drank almost every night, a minimum of seven pints of strong cider. I smoked like a train. I could not go to sleep unless I'd smoked a joint. I remember I use to feel myself coming down from the effects of the drugs after a night out, and I *knew* that there was more to life. I always knew that there were other ways to enjoy life, and I wanted to experience natural happiness. All I really wanted, was a stable home, and for real life to start.

I gave up all of the drugs, smoking and drinking within mine and Steve's first official week together. We were talking one night, and I was leaning out of our bedroom window, smoking a cigarette. Living in Cornwall is so peaceful at night. In all of the homes I have lived in since I have been here in Cornwall, the clear night has always been so tranquil. You can hear the owls, and the sky on a clear night is lit up with thousands of stars. When it is a clear night, It is a completely clear sky; there is no city smog.

I exhaled out into the night air and looked up at Steve, who was sitting in our bed looking at the TV. He noticed me looking at him, and we smiled at each other. I asked him if there was anything he'd change about me. He looked thoughtful, in a teasing way. And then said: 'Absolutely nothing. Apart from the smoking. It's like kissing an ashtray.'

I hated the thought that he felt like that every time I went to kiss him. I had flashbacks to being the ugly teenager with smelly breath. I wanted to kiss him whenever I wanted, and for him to enjoy it. How long can a person put up with kissing an ashtray? What if he recoils in disgust one day when I go to kiss him? Shit, that would break my heart.

I quit. And that was it. I haven't smoked since. I've been completely clear of fags, and daily drinking, and drugs, for almost fourteen years. It was really hard at first, because giving up that lifestyle meant that I couldn't see my usual crowd of friends. I am not sure if I have ever explained to them why I just disappeared and disconnected like that, but it was because I didn't trust myself to not go back to that sort of lifestyle. I may have seemed happy when I was that party girl, but it didn't satisfy the needs of my inner soul, and the life that I truly craved. I yearned for a calm, stable haven, and a soul mate to share it with.

I loved working in QA. The role was varied, and I got to work on different shifts with different people, regularly. Every day I had different issues to sort out, new problems to solve or investigate. I loved the challenge of learning on the job and managing my own time and work routine. My new boss, Kate, was amazing, and I could not have admired her any more than I did. She could teach me anything, by breaking everything down into very simple terms and small, bite-sized chunks. She made things click inside my head like no one ever had before. She was a total role model for me. Until the day came that she was moving to a new role, and we had a new manager. Kate had set the bar pretty high for any new manager I would ever have again.

After four years in QA, that familiar feeling started to creep in. Whenever I imagined working at this factory for all of my working years, or for any other company, for that matter, I felt extremely demotivated and depressed. I could not accept that thought. I had this inner feeling, which I can only describe as a 'knowing', that I was capable of more, that I wanted to do something for myself. I wanted to be my own boss.

In 2006, Steve came home from work with a second-hand laptop. I was extremely bored, and looking for a hobby. I discovered eBay, and, wow! I was hooked. A selling platform, where I could list anything for sale, and the whole world could potentially see it, and I could just sell it and send it? Shit. The. Bed! I cleared every cupboard, draw, wardrobe, nook and cranny in the entire house. There *was* no hoard by the time I'd finished selling all of our priceless crap on eBay. Pretty soon, Steve was getting pissed off with things being sold from under his feet, and threatened to start bolting things down if I didn't stop.

I'd started to get to know the local postmaster, what with all the posting I was doing. He ran the post office from the back of his shop, and the front of the shop was an empty shell, apart from a couple of card stands. It was the only shop on its particular section of road, and the only customers it saw were the locals wanting to draw their pension, post something, pay a bill or buy a greeting card.

I started to realise that if I wanted to make a living on eBay, I needed the stock to sell. But what? Where on earth would I get the stock, and how on earth would I decide what to sell? I started looking for job lots of cheap stuff on eBay. Looking back now, we didn't half buy some crap. Pallets of electrical goods, to break down and sell off separately on eBay. We nearly always lost money by doing this, as the postage of any items sold on eBay often made the product too expensive for our customers to buy. Pretty soon, I had the idea to sell items on eBay on behalf of the public, charging a 20% commission on the final selling price of each item. We had a house full of boxes upon boxes of the dodgy job lots I'd bought from eBay. There were also countless items given to us by local people, who were hoping for massive returns on the rubber band ball they'd spent the last ten years making, or the interestingly shaped pieces of driftwood they'd found on the beach. One man's piece of rubbish is another man's treasure!

I was still working in QA at Tamarfoods and had earned the nickname 'Delgirl'. (Delgirl is derived from the TV character Delboy, of *Only Fools and*

HAND TO MOUTH

Horses. One of his favourite catch phrases was "This time next year; we'll be millionaires".)

On days off I would sit in the canteen, selling Christmas cards at Christmas time, or end of season costume jewellery from high street retailers at any other time. I even convinced the local pub to allow me to throw jewellery parties, and I would cover their pool table with a sheet, and then display all the costume jewellery at mega cheap prices.

The postmaster made us an amazing offer one day and gave us permission to use his empty shop as our base, to run our eBay business. I handed in my notice at Tamarfoods and left to work in the shop. I was so excited!

The local press came out to take photos of me standing proudly outside the shop, interviewing me about our new service, which we called 'Sellforall'. We registered our new business as BOB Enterprises. Unofficially, the BOB stood for all of our surname initials, which was obviously me, Steve and the postmaster, but officially it was supposed to mean Bronzed or broadband. By the time we opened, we had a stand-up tanning booth, as well as the eBay selling service, internet access and costume jewellery. I also started importing job lots of fine jewellery from the US (the exchange rate at the time was around $1.87 to £1) and from China and India, which I would then get hallmarked at the Birmingham assay office. Looking back, it was such a strange setup, a real mishmash of products and services. I had no idea how to market any of it at the time, so I was relying on the footfall into the shop, which was mostly pensioners.

After eighteen months of trying, we had to admit to ourselves that this business venture wasn't going anywhere. And definitely not as fast as we needed it to. I felt extreme guilt that Steve was working every hour of overtime that he could to support us both, as well as relying heavily on credit cards and an overdraft, and I just wasn't bringing in any extra money at all. We were broke, and Steve had been made bankrupt.

The stress took its toll, and I was diagnosed with severe depression and anxiety. It was the worst thing that I had ever experienced. I would not wish depression on anyone. Not even Poohy McPoohface, who you will read about later on. At my lowest point, I wanted to sink below the water in my bath one night but cried because I knew I didn't have the bottle to do it. I wanted to run head first at a wall, knock myself out, and not wake up at all. I felt totally and utterly empty, hollow, and desperately lonely, even when surrounded by loved ones. I avoided calling my family in Coventry or spending time with close friends. I didn't feel anything. I just questioned my existence and felt everything was entirely pointless. I didn't care about anything. I couldn't make even the simplest of decisions.

The doctor offered anti-depressants, and I refused them. I don't disagree with people taking them, not at all, but I'd seen my parents and other members of my family relying on them for long periods of time, so I struggled to see the long-term benefits. I saw them as a mask, rather than treating the problem at its root. I'm by no means an expert on how to treat depression, but I knew that I wanted to equip myself with the mental tools to keep depression at bay for the rest of my life.

I sat down with Steve, and we made a plan. We decided that he would become my brain crutch. He would also be my confidante, my listener. I would talk to him at least once a day about how I was feeling so that he was always on the same page as me. He would make all decisions for me, on my behalf, seeing as though even deciding what to have for tea was too much for me. We joined the gym, and we were very strict about going three times a week. We closed down BOB

HAND TO MOUTH

Enterprises, and I went back to work at Tamarfoods, this time as an operative on the shop floor. It was just what I needed.

I didn't want any responsibility, I needed the physical work and for someone to just point and say: 'Do this, that and the other.' I did as I was told, I had a routine back, and I was sleeping much better. There was finally some space in my brain to spend on nothing but resting.

I loved work after a while. The freedom of knowing I had a full-time wage coming in was enough to make me feel grateful, happy, and like some of the weight had been lifted. No doubt the exercise from the hard, physical work was helping too.

For the two-year recovery period, the depression still sat on my shoulders, constantly whispering in my ears: 'Wow, this is all very strange. Look how far away everyone is. They're right beside you. Right in front of you. But *so* far away. Look how detached you are. Can you feel how numb you are inside? You really don't care, do you? Not that you don't care, but you don't *not* care, either. You don't feel *anything*. And no one even knows. You're so alone.'

One of the parts of my recovery plan was learning some Cognitive Behavioural Therapy and reading a couple of self-help books. One of the books was written by a psychologist called Claire Weeks. This book saved me. One sentence from that book, made complete sense of how I was feeling, in turn making me realise that I wasn't alone, that other people had felt, and did feel the same.

We decided that whenever I had very strong, upsetting feelings, I would just allow them to pass. I'd observe them, acknowledge them, and then just wait for them to pass, like a cloud. I didn't try to force myself to feel better, or get better, or ignore them. I just rode out the feelings until, at some point, around eighteen months later, the worst feelings no longer felt as frightening. We'd started making plans to concentrate on, and those plans, plus going to the gym and eating a lot healthier, all worked to slowly help me heal. There were lots of other things that helped of course, such as talking, and talking, and talking, every single day, to Steve. He made sure we didn't miss that part.

After two years, I was more or less healed, although the anxiety never completely went away. We started trying for a baby. Early in 2010, we found out we were expecting. Unfortunately, the pregnancy was ectopic, leading obviously to miscarriage at seven weeks.

HAND TO MOUTH

After a week, I was back at work, when I experienced a huge amount of blood loss. I was taken into hospital and examined, and it was decided I'd suffered a miscarriage of suspected twins, but somehow they'd missed the location of the second one. We were absolutely gutted but decided to carry on trying. Within a few months, I was pregnant again. The doctors were very vigilant, scanning me at six weeks to ensure the baby was in the correct place this time and thankfully, he was. I could never seem to muster the same feelings of elation with this second pregnancy. I'd been so utterly devastated at the failure of our first pregnancy that I was too scared to get my hopes up.

HAND TO MOUTH

Chapter 4. Babies, socks and GERD.

James, AKA Jimmy, came into the world in March 2011. I was not good at being pregnant. I was an evil nutcase. I didn't like being around anyone, I didn't like having to talk, and I hated anyone touching my bump. I'd go to work with the best fuck off face I could muster, willing everyone to just stay away from me. I did nothing, but complain about how much pain I was in. I seemed to be in constant pain with my pelvis and hips, so I wasn't sleeping well, and my hormones seemed to be all over the place. The only thing I really loved was feeling our little bundle moving around inside me. Poor Steve. What a nightmare it must've been, putting up with my constant moaning.

We decided we didn't want to know the sex of the baby until D-Day. This made it all so much more exciting. A small part of me was sort of hoping for a girl. I'm not sure why, I think I just imagined playing with girl stuff and being girly girls together. We'd agreed on the name Charlotte for a girl, but neither of us could think of a boys' name that we both liked.

HAND TO MOUTH

A couple of months before the baby was due; I suddenly realised I really wanted to have the same surname as my little one when they entered the world. Steve and I were engaged and had been for around seven years. I had never been one to dream of getting married or a big white wedding. Almost everyone I knew, that had been married, had split up. I didn't have a lot of faith in marriage and thought it an old-fashioned idea.

However, I did want us all to have the same surname. We agreed to just get it done, simply and cheaply, while I was pregnant. We got married in a registry office, with both of our parents present and no one else. I was eight months pregnant. We left the registry office, went home, I got changed into my pyjamas, and we ordered a Chinese. It was perfect.

On the night I went into labour, we had snuggled up in bed to watch a film when I suddenly felt a pop. As I got out of bed to go to the toilet and check to see if there was anything going on, my waters trickled down my legs, and all over the carpet, and I left a trail of wet footprints all the way to the toilet. I laughed, and laughed, and excitedly shouted to Steve, "it's happening, it's happening, my waters have broken!! OMG, we're going to meet our baby!"

HAND TO MOUTH

I sat on the toilet, and while waiting for the waters to stop trickling, I called my Mum, still laughing my head off. She was getting ready to go out with my Auntie Sarah, and she couldn't believe I was laughing. Steve and I got into the car and went off to the hospital. I had learned simple meditation while recovering from the depression and decided to use the breathing practices during my labour.

When we got to the hospital, I got out at the maternity reception and waited for Steve to park the car. I was having contractions while waiting for him, and I just couldn't stop laughing with excitement. When we were shown to our delivery room, our midwife came in and introduced herself as Charlotte. Steve and I exchanged looks, grinning, and we joked how it must be a sign. Charlotte's shift came to an end, and we were still nowhere near ready to birth baby Boothby. The next midwife took over, also called Charlotte. Steve and I exchanged looks again. This was *totally* going to be a girl!!

Eighteen hours after we got to the hospital, our little Jimmy entered the world. He was placed on my stomach, and my whole world changed forever. That moment, made me feel more complete in a way that nothing else ever had, and I finally felt like my life had a total purpose. Everything else in my life made sense, and I felt so unbelievably proud, loved up, and utterly blessed. I felt like a lioness, and this was my cub, and he was mine to love, nurture, and protect, no matter what. To say I felt protective of Jimmy was an understatement. I felt all of this before I even checked to see what was between this baby's legs. When I looked, I just laughed. It didn't matter what sex my baby was. This baby was already the best thing that had ever happened to me, and I wouldn't have swapped a million babies for this one in my arms.

The next few months were a whirlwind of nappies, constant puking and what we *thought* was colic. Jimmy was sick, like, *constantly*. No one seemed to believe, or realise, just how bad it was at first, apart from Steve obviously, seeing as he was there to witness it and help clean it up. With my parents and family being so far away, there were few people we felt we could call on for help. Most people would listen to me go on about how I'd had to change him for the seventh time that day and nod politely, making comments such as: 'Well that's babies for you!' Whether they thought I was exaggerating, I'm not sure. My Mum came to stay for a while and saw first-hand what it was like. It was endless, and we realised that something else was up; this was not just your typical baby vomiting.

HAND TO MOUTH

After a lot of doctor visits and hospital trips, Jimmy was diagnosed with GERD. This is a form of acid reflux that meant his stomach contents could flow back up into his throat and out of his mouth at any moment. He was prescribed Domperidone and Omeprazole which we had to administer a few times a day. My grandparents were on these medications for acid indigestion, which made it feel even more serious.

The GERD was so bad, Jimmy would have attacks of what appeared to be some kind of seizure, and even foamed at the mouth and choked a couple of times. This was explained as Sandifer Syndrome eventually, which is associated with symptomatic gastroesophageal reflux, amongst other conditions. I called the ambulance a couple of times when he choked. By the time the ambulance turned up, he would be fine, and I would feel like an idiot. The first responders and the ambulance staff were very supportive and friendly, understanding you cannot be too careful where babies are concerned. Even so, I would feel like a neurotic Mum and feared them not believing me if it happened again. I'm sure that these events all helped my anxiety to return and with a vengeance.

To make matters a little worse, Jimmy was constantly trying to ram his whole hand into his mouth. This made the skin on his hands sore, and he would make himself gag. Gagging, for Jimmy, *meant* being sick, because his oesophagus was not strong enough to keep his stomach contents down where they should have stayed. The hand chewing exacerbated the problem.

I know a lot of Mums, Dads, parents and carers will identify a lot with some of the things I've already written about babies so far, but I think almost everyone understands what it is like that first time you wake up and find horrible, bloody scratches across your baby's face. Their little fingernails are like razors, and obviously the more they wriggle when they have not mastered fine motor control, the more likely they are to scratch themselves. We'd bought a lot of anti-scratch mittens, but they never stayed on. And while I'm on that subject, why are they called scratch mitts? They're *anti*-scratch mitts, aren't they? Regardless, they did not work, so I had started putting his socks on his hands instead. They worked a treat, and my Mummy friends were doing that, too.

HAND TO MOUTH

Chapter 5. A light bulb, Sophie, and Alibaba.

Jimmy had over twenty teething toys and teethers. I was frustrated that he obviously needed some kind of oral stimulation, for whatever reason, but that he was far too young to actually grasp a traditional teething toy. Surely there was something on the market that was specifically designed for young babies, to give them a little more control?

After a few Google searches, Sophie the Giraffe kept popping up. Sophie was launched in the 60's and was the world's number one teether at the time. I was glad to have found these results, as our close friends Gareth and Kate (Kate being my ex-boss from the factory job I'd had in QA at Tamarfoods, and now Technical Manager at Gummee) had bought Jimmy a Sophie the Giraffe. Sophie's slender limbs are designed to be easy to hold for babies. That was great, and Jimmy did laugh his little head off when he heard her squeak and would smile at her pretty face, but he still didn't have the dexterity to bring her to his mouth to chew on.

HAND TO MOUTH

I could not get my head around the fact that everyone I spoke to, health professionals included, were all aware that babies don't have the dexterity to actually grasp a teething toy until they're around five to six months old. I couldn't believe that humans had known this, since the dawn of time, and yet there wasn't a product that could be attached to the baby's hand, for the purpose of teething.

One day, I was changing Jimmy's nappy in the nursery. He had socks on his hands, and I remember thinking he'd been unusually quiet and content for the last couple of hours. He was a very content baby, apart from the GERD episodes, but on this day I'd also been convinced that he was starting to teethe because he was a little unsettled and his cheeks were flushed. I glanced up and noticed he had managed to wiggle some excess of the sock, at the tips of his fingers, and he was having a good old suck and chew on this sock. I immediately thought; 'He needs a teething mitten!'

"Honey!" I shouted. Steve was in the living room. "Can you Google Teething Mitten? And get him one, please? I think he'd absolutely love it; it's exactly what he needs!"

A few minutes went by.

HAND TO MOUTH

"There's no such thing, honey," came Steve's reply. It still had not occurred to me, at that point, that teething mittens might not exist. I decided to myself that perhaps he'd not been as thorough in his search efforts as I would have been, and I'd have a look as soon as I had time. Over the next few days and weeks, I was stunned to discover that there was no such thing as a teething mitten. It seemed like such an obvious idea! What I did find, however, were posts in Mother and baby forums, from Mums, Dads and carers, asking if anyone knew if there was such a thing as a teether that could be attached to the hand. I also found a patent application for a teething mitten from 1952 by a woman called Martha Ann Bryson, but it had not been granted, and no product had ever been launched. I started to get excited. That familiar, entrepreneurial spirit was stirring, whirring with idea's and enthusiasm. OMG. I'd found a waiting market. And no product. I knew I had to look into it.

Unfortunately, we were bankrupt. We had *zero* funds. Apart from the baby stuff, we were buying everything from the Tesco Value range to help our budget stretch further. I decided there must be a way to just look into it, using the internet. I'd done the basic, usual Google searches, which is how I'd found the application for a teething mitten in 1952, by Martha Ann Bryson.

HAND TO MOUTH

Steve had been issued with a special type of credit card, one of those that has an extortionate interest rate but is designed to help you build your credit rating back up. It had a limit of £500 on it. I contacted an innovation company to find out how much it would cost to have a worldwide patent and product search done. It would cost £500.

I explained this to Steve, and he gave me a look. The sort of look that a husband would give after he'd already experienced the roller coaster of entrepreneurial ventures that his Del-girl wife had already dragged him through. He handed me the card and said: "Honey. This. Is. The. Last. Time. If this does not work, there can be *no more* of these crazy business ventures. *Promise me!*"

I knew he was totally justified, and I hesitated. I took the card and sat down in an armchair in our living room. I thought about my idea, and I closed my eyes. I imagined walking into a baby shop, a year, two years down the line. I imagined seeing a teething mitten on the shelf, one *not* launched by me. I couldn't stand that thought. I *had* to give it a try. After all, being an entrepreneur means taking risks, it's exciting, and all part of the thrill!

Because if, *what if*…..it all pays off?

HAND TO MOUTH

Looking back, I think even if I'd decided not to do anything, I would definitely have reached another point in life where, no matter what, that inner Del-girl would have needed a vent.

I paid the innovation company and impatiently waited for the results of their search. What I received in the post a few weeks later, was basically a print out of everything I had already found on the internet. They'd also added a small bit of 'market research', which was just whatever the birth rate was for the year before. The report said that in 2012, there were 79,000 babies born. I'd already discovered that the actual number was 790,000. I should have complained, but when you have an idea for a new product, and you're convinced it will work, you worry that someone will steal your idea, and who has more resources and experience than innovation companies? I felt we'd pretty much wasted £500, and for incorrect information to boot. I was gutted. No more funds left to chase this dream. I promised Steve I would leave it at that. But, of course, I couldn't.

I spoke to more innovation companies in the UK, to find out if there was any way we could work with one. Even if I could get some helpful hints and tips from them, it was worth a shot. One company sent me their non-disclosure agreement, and I signed it and sent it back. Upon doing so, they had promised to send me their feedback and advice about where to go from there.

Here was their reply, upon receiving my email, detailing my idea: (I have removed all names and details, to protect their identity and of course to comply with the legal paperwork that we had all signed.)

Jodine

Thanks for your text – don't worry everything received with thanks.

Our feedback for you:

We understand the idea and quite like it. However, we have reservations about the concept as it is.
Firstly, without a patent, you could pursue a registered design, but we do not believe this would be enough to sell or licence the idea.

The second issue is hygiene. As a mitt or glove, we feel this is an issue. Whatever scheme is used it cannot get and stay wet or even damp, and it needs to be readily sanitised as I am sure you are aware.

HAND TO MOUTH

So we like the idea but not the current execution. What we think you need is a re-think on how to deliver the function you are looking for via an alternative execution, the development of a nice brand name and a detailed review of the relevant product and testing standards.

If you wanted to go and sell it from here (licence or otherwise) you would probably need prototypes and test results. You could then take it to a company or direct to Mothercare and pitch it.

This would take a reasonable sum of money I am afraid and I very sorry to hear that what you did have sounds to have been wasted by another design company. We certainly would not feel comfortable if you had to sell precious possession to finance us.

This is only our opinion of course, but I am not sure what else to suggest from here. Perhaps you could talk to MAS (www.mymas.org) to see whether there is any matched funding available? It might take a bit of the sting out of a small project. One point of caution is the new MAS is all about growth and companies rather than inventors or start-ups so it may be prudent to research and consider the requirements before you approach them should you choose to do so.

HAND TO MOUTH

I hope this helps.'

Although appreciative of their thoughts and their time, I was quite disheartened to read the email, and it was almost enough to put me off. I mulled it over for a few days. I wondered if we could get a registered design but not a patent, why would I not then be able to sell it?

I wasn't looking to licence it; I just wanted to make it and sell the product, not the idea. I wanted to be in control of the whole thing. Like the determined little control freak that I am. I was confused at first, by that sentence; that they didn't believe a registered design would be enough to sell the idea or licence it. Now, of course, reading it more than five years on, it makes sense. I never did want to sell the idea or license it to anyone. I wanted to launch my *own* product and my *own* business.

Now though, I have learned so much more. Licensing a product idea is hard. Or even selling it, if that is all you have, *just* the idea, and nothing else, the buyer would have all the leverage. However, if your idea is a proven product and your brand is well-known and respected, that is different. But as I said, I was none the wiser back then.

HAND TO MOUTH

Their point about hygiene confused the hell out of me. A teether cannot get or stay wet. I had plush toys, teddy bears and other toys made of soft, absorbent materials that were designed for babies to teethe on, and yet their label stated 'HAND WASH ONLY'. All of the literature I was given at the time by health officials, said that everything that is intended for babies to place in the mouth had to be sterilised before use. And yet, there were teethers on the market that said hand wash only? How confusing.

I spoke to a couple of midwives and did some research; checking all of Jimmy's teethers and their washing instructions. All of them said that they had to be washed in warm soapy water. Bingo! I really, honestly felt that the innovation company that wrote me that email, were wrong in their opinion about the hygiene and execution of my product.

I spoke to another innovation company, and over a quick chat on the phone, they worked out that to get us to the point where we'd have Computer Aided Designs, Intellectual Property registrations, Safety testing, a website, proper market research, possible retailer interest and a few prototypes, we were looking at around

HAND TO MOUTH

£50,000. We didn't even have £50. And there certainly wasn't anyone we knew that would invest that sort of money in just an idea.

Back to the drawing board.

That night, I could not sleep. I was doing it again - imagining what it would be like to walk into Mothercare and see my idea, designed and launched by someone else, sitting on the shelf. I wracked my brains. How was I going to do this? What could I possibly do, to turn this into a reality? What could I do on my own, that might convince someone that I'd proven it to be a sure-fire hit, enough to convince them to invest? What resources had I used when I imported the jewellery?

I suddenly remembered how I'd found the manufacturers of the jewellery I had imported, on alibaba.com. Surely there would be manufacturers listed on there, that could help me with my idea. It was 1am.

I got out of bed and headed to my computer in the living room. I logged in, and as if by some sort of telepathic ability, Jimmy started to cry. I went to his cot, lifted him out and warmed a bottle. With Jimmy on my lap, all snuggled in after his bottle; I scoured the listings for manufacturers that looked as though they could make what I had in mind. I found over two hundred profiles of manufacturers that looked as though they could make the product. I sifted through them all, selecting sixty that ticked all of the boxes, from great feedback to up-to-date factory audits and safety certificates.

My message read:

'Hi there,
 My name is Jodine Boothby and I have designed a teething product for babies. I have applied for the design right in the UK. When it is granted, could you possibly make the prototype if I send you the design illustrations? And also give me a quote on manufacture costs?
Kind regards
J Boothby'

Obviously, I had not applied for a design right at that stage, but they weren't to know. For anyone that doesn't know, a design right is basically just a way of protecting the way your product looks; it means that no one can copy your exact design of a product.

Unfortunately, because of the patent applications that I'd found, from Martha Ann Bryson, a teething mitt was not considered to be a new idea and was therefore not patentable. I'd called lots of different solicitors and patent attorneys in the UK and the USA, and most of them give you around thirty minutes advice for free on your first introduction or call. I wrote down everything I needed to know, and I called as many as I could, to get as much information as possible. That way I could make a half-educated decision about what to do. Martha Ann Bryson's patent application, though not granted, was considered to be prior art. The manufacturers that I emailed knew nothing about me. How were they to know I wasn't loaded and could afford all the legal stuff you could shake a stick at?

By the time I'd emailed them, it was 5am. I was so excited; I didn't feel tired. It felt like another step had been taken. Maybe, whatever they came back with, was doable? By 9am on that very same morning, I'd had a reply from one of the companies I'd emailed. They quoted $200, for a team of them to work on my product, and I would get six samples in the post. That worked out at the time to be around £120 - back when the exchange rate was a lot more favourable. I had some silver jewellery left over from my jewellery business, as well as a couple of white gold Tanzanite rings that I'd planned on keeping as heirlooms to pass down through the family. I decided to sell it all on eBay, to raise the funds to pay the factory to

HAND TO MOUTH

work on my prototypes. One of the Tanzanite rings had a valuation certificate, as I'd recently had it valued, for £1500. I sold it for £115. I was so upset, but I believed in my product idea so much, I just kept focusing on that. There would be other times in my life that I'd be able to collect heirlooms to be passed on.

I raised what I needed, but I knew I couldn't just tell them my idea without some protection, or guarantee. I knew I had to send the factory some legal paperwork to sign, to agree that they would not disclose my idea to any third party, or use my idea for any other means than those intended. I couldn't afford to pay a solicitor to issue me with my own specific paperwork, however, I did call a solicitor and found out that what I needed was called a non-disclosure agreement. Google outdid itself again, and offered me lots of free, basic templates. I changed the wording a little, and sent it, with fingers crossed, to the factory.

I figured that they'd think I obviously knew what I was doing, and had money to spend, so they'd take me seriously. Plus, I was willing to risk it. What choice did I have? They signed it and sent it back to me. We were ready to start.

I had already asked them if they would accept hand-drawn designs instead of computer-aided

HAND TO MOUTH

designs, and they had no problem with that. All the innovation companies I'd spoken to had said that I absolutely, definitely, would need Computer Aided Designs. It would have cost us around £200 to get those done, and again, it was £200 that we just did not have. I set to work on my drawings. Project Teetha Mitt, as I'd originally wanted to call it, was a go!

This is the first ever sketch, or design, of what would become the world's first, commercially available teething mitten. I sent this, plus views

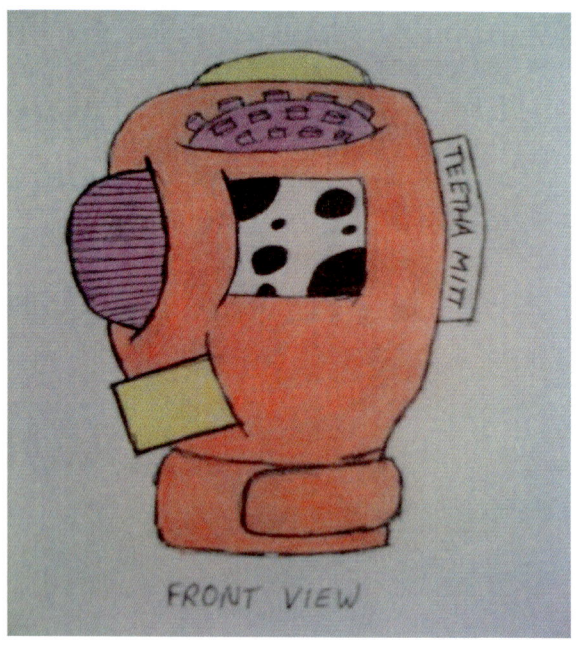

of the back and sides, to my new manufacturers and explained what I wanted. The date was 13/01/2012.

By the end of March 2012, I had the six samples I'd been promised, and I was over the moon. By now, I'd roped in Lucy, one of the friends I'd become close to while working at Tamarfoods. I'd also handed in my notice at Tamarfoods, as while on maternity leave with Jimmy, the shift patterns had been changed and there was no way that Steve and I could both stay employed there and find childcare for the times that our shifts crossed over.

I'd met Lucy not long after I first started at Tamarfoods, back in 2000. I was standing next to her on the handline, where around twenty women hand crimped Cornish pasties all day long. I'd never spoken to her before and found her intimidatingly popular, funny, and confident. On this particular day, Lucy screamed into my ear: "Will you just shut the fuck up?"

I was shocked and opened my mouth, but nothing would come out. "Hey?! What?"

Everyone was looking at me and laughing. Lucy burst out laughing, and I realised this was Lucy's way of breaking the ice. We've been besties ever since. Lucy, although having witnessed all of my other dodgy Delgirl ventures, fully supported me, from concept to prototype. She came to our house every Wednesday night, for a couple of hours, while we discussed and planned project Teetha Mitt.

The weekend after we received our prototypes, Lucy and I exhibited at the Cornwall Baby Fair in Falmouth, Cornwall. I spoke a few times with the manager of the show and opened up to her about my worries over whether or not my product would be liked, or even understood. At around the same time, I was feeling and experiencing some familiar symptoms. Something far more important was happening.

I did a pregnancy test and was shocked to find it was positive. I wondered how the hell we were going to launch our new product and business, around raising our two babies. Oh shit. I was over the moon but scared about how we'd cope. We were nervous, but we went along and set up our little table at the Cornwall Baby Fair in Falmouth, in March 2012. I was so nervous I felt sick, and couldn't figure out whether it was nerves or morning sickness.

The response we received for Gummee glove was amazing. I should mention at this point, that we'd realised we could not register the trademark 'Teetha Mitt', as it was just too general. It would not offer much protection for us legally, in the long run. It would have been a bit like trying to register the word 'Car', as a trademark if you wanted to launch your own car design. I asked on my personal Facebook page if anyone had any suggestions for what we should call the glove, and my sister-in-law, Jenny, suggested Gummi Glove. I loved it, but the word Gummi was being used for something else. I looked for variations of the spelling and found that the word Gummee was not being used by anyone, at least not in the class that we would be registering, which was in toys and pacifiers.

At the show, we were surprised to find that a lot of Mothers-to-be, who were visiting the show and had no other children, did not understand the product, or the need for it.

However, their own Mother, the grandmother-to-be, understood it completely. We took seventeen direct orders, even though they knew we'd have no stock at least until May. We also took four wholesale orders from nursery shops that were exhibiting. Charged by the excitement that we'd proved there was a market, I took to the stage at the event, to explain who I was and what my invention was. I was terrified to stand up there, in front of so many people, and speak publicly for the first time. The show organiser thrust a glass of champagne into my hand when she realised that I was actually considering making a run for it, and it seemed to help.

Thank you to Angie Stanforth, for your help and encouragement on that day!

HAND TO MOUTH

Chapter 6: For the love of gLOVE

We had to raise the cash we needed, and fast, now that we had orders to fulfil. I worked hard, putting together an awesome business plan. I had no idea what I was doing; I'd never prepared a business plan before. I couldn't do cash flow charts or forecasts! There was no money to even start with, or base the financials on, so off I went, on a wing and a prayer, to the first bank on our list of banks to hit. NatWest. It was funny, at the time, the amount of people that said: "Ooh, the banks will help you financially! They have been told they need to start helping small businesses!" Not true. We went to every bank. They all loved my business plan and the product. However, the decision was always based on the same thing; our personal financial situation. If your personal credit rating is bad, you're not going to get any help from any high street bank for a business idea. Funnily enough though, one of the banks still tried to sell us a business bank account, even knowing our situation.

We were so fortunate and humbled by how many of our friends and family helped us, financially. My Mum sold her car, my Nan Sylve loaned us money, and some of our closest friends lent us money from their savings. We managed to borrow enough to pay for the first production run, and the product testing.

While waiting for the first production run to be completed, I started work on our online presence. First came the website, which I managed to set up on Vistaprint. It cost very little; I think around £20 per month, and about £2 for our domain name, which was www.gummeeglove.co.uk. I couldn't believe I was actually doing it. Someone had recently quoted around £10,000 to build our website, and here I was, creating my own, for stupid, *stupid* money! A website, where my product could attract not only customers in the UK but internationally too? My very own shop, online? It felt crazy and unbelievably exciting.

2012. Social media for business was just starting to take off, and, in the UK at least, people were just starting to talk about how it was going to be the future of business advertising. Much larger companies, the massive brands that had been around for many years, were still trundling along using their traditional advertising media and routes to market. New businesses were realising the massive potential of social media when used correctly. I remembered back to 2007, when Facebook was still brand new to the UK, and I was trying to convince all my friends to join after one of my oldest and best friends, Nik, had convinced me to join it. I had a friend on there who was in my class at secondary school, called Troy. I remember him posting how businesses were going to realise one day that social media was going to be the future. I read it, totally didn't understand, and dismissed it as nerd speak (sorry Troy!) Obviously, it wasn't nerd speak, and he was right.

Troy was in my tutor group throughout secondary school, but we barely spoke two words to one another. I remember once our drama teacher, for some mad reason, paired us all off and we had to go somewhere quiet in the school and discuss, and I think write down, what we would be doing in the future if we were a couple. Very bizarre exercise and I've no idea what the point of it was, but I'd been paired up with Troy. We had both said how we would be running our own businesses. Troy is also now an entrepreneur.

To prepare for our launch, I set up a Facebook page for Gummee glove, and other than asking all of my friends to like and share, I had no idea how to utilise it until our official launch.

HAND TO MOUTH

Around this time, we were trying to figure out how to advertise, where to advertise, and how we could get free publicity. We certainly had no budget for advertising.

Lucy, Gummee's Lucy, as she is now known, was still helping us. At our house, every Wednesday without fail, for at least a couple of hours, as we planned our next steps. She had two children of her own and was still working her day job.

Lucy mentioned a girl she had gone to school with, called Sam, and explained that Sam was a journalist who might be able to help. She messaged her, and then passed her email on to me. Sam, amazingly, agreed to help us. She wrote press releases for us and sent them off to local press offices and newspapers, local TV news shows and radio stations. Both of the main local TV news shows wanted to come and interview me, which was very exciting but absolutely nerve-wracking, too. ITV West Country and BBC Spotlight South West came out to interview me in the same week. We saw a spike in sales then, in the South West. Our story was in all of the local newspapers, which we were then able to use on social media and on our website, all adding credibility to us, our product and our brand. It really helped to raise the Gummee glove profile.

HAND TO MOUTH

Our launch date was looming, and our very first production run arrived just two days before the show. We were in such a panic, we'd paid around £2000 for the stand, and we had people to re-pay, this *had* to work! Our stand looked like something from a school fete, looking back at photos of it now, but we were so proud of it at the time. We were surrounded by huge, professional stand builds and well-known industry brands, yet there we were, with our humble pasting table, bed sheet tablecloth (un-ironed) and handmade bunting all over the place. You have to start somewhere! We didn't even have packaging for Gummee glove, so we sold them in little plastic yellow bags, with an A4 info sheet inserted into it.

We'd had an email from Donal Macintyre's PA just before the show, asking if we could offer any samples for his son, Hunter. He walked past our stand and didn't stop, so I chased him, introduced myself and he very kindly came back to the stand, had a selfie with me, and I gave him a Gummee glove for baby Hunter. This was our first celebrity claim to fame.

We sold one hundred and forty-four units over the course of the weekend, and during the show, Lucy had the awesome idea of introducing the 'Face of Gummee' competition on the Facebook page. We would ask parents to submit photos of their babies using a Gummee glove. We would share them on our Facebook page and whichever photo had the most likes by the end of the month would be our 'Face of Gummee glove' for the whole of the following month. It was a massive hit, right from the very start. Facebook back then was yet to impose restrictions on business pages, so whoever liked your page, saw your posts, too. It ran like a dream, with parents furiously sharing their baby's photo's using the Gummee glove. It was amazing, and so very humbling, and unbelievable, seeing so many photos of babies using and enjoying a product that I had invented.

We broke even at the show, which Steve was not too happy about. He was (is) Gummee's accountant and finance manager, or as I like to call him, number understanderer. He wanted to see profit straight away. I remember trying to explain that to break even at a show like that, when we looked so amateur, as well as being a brand-new product and brand, was pretty damn good. We have also learned since that a lot of value is held in the exposure of the brand and product to so many people visiting the show, whether they buy or not.

We thought about how to get the product out there, using other means. Any sort of advertising that did not cost the earth, but would work. I had

HAND TO MOUTH

*Gummee glove's launch, NEC 2012.
Gummee's Lucy featured.*

no idea how to do marketing, none of us had any experience at all. All we could do was put ourselves in the mindset of the person that would be most likely to come looking for a teether. Mums, parents, grandparents and carers. One of the first companies I could think of was Bounty. Every mum gets a Bounty folder when she is pregnant. Or at least they did when I had my two, and I was in early stages of pregnancy with Charlie. I called them, and they offered us an amazing opportunity. They were just about to start email flash sales. Companies would offer a discount on certain products for a limited time, and Bounty would email the offer out to their database of over half a million Mums, over the course of a week.

We went ahead with this deal with Bounty. The first day came, and the first email didn't go out until 6pm that night. I received the email, seeing as I was already in their database. We could not believe what happened next. Steve and I both had our phones set to ring out like a cash register, every time we had a sale through Paypal. Our phones started going off, and at one point that night, we were selling a glove a minute. It was unreal, and we were dancing all around the living room. I called my Mum and my Dad, excitedly giggling my head off at the sound of the pings in my ear while I was talking to them. I posted all about it on my own personal Facebook page and must have driven everyone crazy with how excited I was, but there was a lot of support. All of my Facebook friends had been watching our journey, right from the very start, when I'd first had the idea. There were times when I wondered whether or not to stop sharing so much, especially during a confidence wobble - which I happen to suffer from frequently. But I felt I wanted to keep everyone up to date, and it was all so exciting, I couldn't *not* share, damn it.

HAND TO MOUTH

The next day we were so busy, packing gloves into boxes ready to be sent, trying to reply to emails that had come in, the phone ringing, while juggling housework and being a Mum. There were boxes all over the house, the only rooms that were unaffected were the bathroom and kitchen. Another email went out on the second day too, and the same thing happened. This pretty much went on every day for the whole week. We were beside ourselves! Just like that, we repaid my Nan. We had to pay everyone off one at a time, as we still needed to pay for more production every time we sold out.

This many gloves being sold in one week meant our Facebook page was crazier than normal, and we saw another huge boost in likes. While all of this was going on, I was being Mum to Jimmy, designing packaging, working part-time at the local newsagents, my bump was growing, and Steve was still working full time at Tamarfoods.

For the rest of 2012, we decided not to do any further shows or anything that cost too much money. We couldn't have done much anyway, what with everything else that was going on. In between working and being a pregnant Mama, I updated the website, Facebook, and made contact with quite a few Mummy bloggers who we sent Gummee glove's to. We were plodding along quite nicely, however still not nicely enough that I could be paid a wage yet.

Jimmy really suffered from teething, and in fact, scrolling my Facebook timeline to try and remember things that happened in late 2012. I can't believe I'd forgotten just how much of a nightmare teething can be, for everyone in the house, and none of us was getting much sleep.

I'd started applying for high profile business awards. Anything I could think of that I could do or apply for, that didn't cost a small fortune, and that might help to raise our profile, I was doing. I applied for the Mumpreneur Awards 2012, which was being held in Warwickshire, just outside of Coventry. This was great, as it meant I could go to the awards ceremony and stay with my Mum, which meant spending time with my family and zero spending on hotels. The application for the Mumpreneur awards was quite a long one, with almost every question in the application requiring an essay style answer. I sat up until the small hours, for a few nights, writing, then rewriting my application. Finally, I sent it off and kept everything crossed. To my absolute astonishment, I received an email a few weeks later to say I was a finalist.

HAND TO MOUTH

The ceremony was held in September 2012. Me, Steve and Jimmy travelled to Coventry and stayed at my Mum's flat. The plan had originally been that my Mum would come with me to the Mumpreneur awards, but my Mum has Fibromyalgia and unfortunately, despite whatever plans you may have, fibromyalgia doesn't care. Poor Mum was having a flare up, and couldn't come with me. I had started talking to an old friend on Facebook, one that I'd come to know at the very first secondary school I went to, called Janet. I asked if she could come instead, and she readily agreed, which was brilliant. Steve stayed home to look after Jimmy.

I'd taken a casual, comfortable dress with me, and some jewellery that I could wear to smarten it up. To my horror, right before we needed to leave my Mums, I realised I didn't have the correct shoes. The only footwear I had bought with me, were my ten-year-old Caterpillar boots (now fifteen years old by the way, and I still *live* in them) and they were battered and worn and *not smart at all*.

Instead of looking the picture of pregnant health and simple elegance that I'd imagined, I looked like I really couldn't be arsed and had just thrown on a potato sack and my dad's work boots. I felt so ashamed as I left the house and got into the car with Janet. She looked so glamorous, and all I kept talking about was how rough I looked and felt.

The Mumpreneur Awards was an amazing setup, with talks and courses being run throughout the day, up until the awards ceremony. It was a great networking opportunity, and to be honest, that was one of the main reasons for me wanting to be there. I wanted to meet other women like me, and find out how they ran their businesses, what marketing tips and information we could swap and share.

The time came to sit and listen to the award announcements. I'd seen and read about previous winners of the Mumpreneur awards, and I had satisfied myself that I was just not of the calibre or standard of those ladies. Despite that, I couldn't stop the internal gut-churning, heart-flipping butterflies. Janet was sitting next to me, and a couple of times leant over, squeezed my arm and kept saying: 'Are you ready?' and 'You're going to win, I know you are!' I just grinned and clapped enthusiastically for the winners being called for the other categories. Then it came to my category, Best New Product. It's not that I didn't have faith in my product. Looking back, I think it was just that I didn't dare to get my hopes up.

HAND TO MOUTH

The moment the photo, of me holding Jimmy and the words 'Gummee Glove' over our heads on the big screen appeared, was an indescribable moment. Janet screamed her head off, I shakily passed her my phone and asked her to take some photos, and my legs just turned to jelly. I welled up while making my way to the stage. Half-way to the stage, looking around at all the lovely big beaming smiles, the finely polished fingernails on the clapping hands, the sparkly dresses and posh hair do's, I suddenly remembered my totally shit attire. Could I get away with it, what with being seven months pregnant? No, not those CAT boots! There was nowhere to hide. I climbed up on the stage, obviously over the moon to have won, and totally humbled, but all of my attention was on the voice inside my head, shouting: 'What the actual fuck have you got on your feet, woman?!'

Part of the award for Best Mumpreneur Product was a six-month contract to supply Gummee glove to Ocado, the online shopping supermarket. We were so excited, and literally felt like we'd almost made it - our first big retailer! Ocado was more of a food supermarket though, and not that it occurred to us at the time, but the minimum spend with Ocado was £40, I guess because it was primarily a food retailer. I had been told that the buyer had agreed to 'hand hold' us, as new suppliers, and help us understand the supply process as well as become a household name. Unfortunately, sales were not good with Ocado. I took it quite badly, though looking back, I understand completely that there were a number of reasons as to why it had not gone well.

Ocado only had a select few baby products within their Nursery section, and our product was not only a new brand that nobody knew, but also a new product and concept. I would advise anyone in the same situation now not to worry, and that it takes time and patience to build a product's reputation and brand. If it's a good product, it will happen eventually, for all the right reasons.

The buyer that I'd spoken to and dealt with left very soon afterwards and the new buyer had not been notified of our special supply arrangement or Mumpreneur win. There had been a couple of mistakes made on our part, and I'd tried to email and call but had no reply. No more orders were made after the initial six-month contract, and I didn't hear a thing from them. This was our first experience of dealing with a large retailer.

Later that year in October 2012, we decided to exhibit at the Baby Show Olympia, in London.

HAND TO MOUTH

Lucy, a friend of ours called Justin (I was almost eight months pregnant and couldn't risk carrying anything remotely heavy in case I went into labour, although secretly, I was hoping that I would go into labour. I couldn't imagine a more perfect setting than a Baby Show, to have a baby! Imagine the publicity!) and of course, me. This would be the show that would give us our first taste of being approached by international buyers.

A buyer for Pottery Barn, USA came to our stand and seemed very keen. This was hugely exciting for me. Looking back from now, to then, I almost want to give me a hug. I was so naive. When I get over the initial cringe, I thank god that things like that used to excite me so much. My naivety spurred my curiosity and fuelled my determination.

During this show, I'd gone off for a break and come back to the stand to find Justin looking really worried. He told me Lucy had just received a call from her Mum, telling her that unfortunately, her brother had passed away. He motioned towards the ladies toilets and said she'd gone in there. I went in to find her, my whole being wanting to wrap her up in a huge cuddle. I could hear her quietly sobbing in one of the cubicles. I called out her name, and while I waited

HAND TO MOUTH

for her to come out, I armed myself with an arm full of tissue and mentally prepared myself for packing everything up and taking Lucy home. Lucy is unbelievably strong, capable, and unflappable. She is fiercely defiant of anything that threatens to knock her down or defeat her, in any way, emotions included. If there was an Einstein version of emotional intelligence, Lucy is it.

Although very sad and upset, Lucy decided to stay, as her Mum had pointed out, what good would it do, getting home early? There was nothing that could be done. I insisted she didn't work, and to just do whatever made her feel comfortable. She went for a walk and met a friend she knew who lived close by.

That night, we went out for a meal and Lucy and Justin had a few drinks. She told us stories about her brother, Mark, and had us in fits of laughter. We went back to our hotel room and spent the evening critiquing our hotel. We were in fits of giggles, in between the sadness. I was amazed, absolutely bowled over, and so full of respect for how Lucy handled that show.

I love you, Lucy. Over the last five years, I have been lucky enough to see through your super strong exterior and into the super soft, squidgy soul that you really are. You're totally awesome.

HAND TO MOUTH

We started to really understand the typical supplier/retailer relationship. Most telephone numbers that you can ever obtain for a buyer unless they have personally given it to you, will just ring. And ring and ring. Sometimes, you'll get the buyer's voicemail, and you can leave a message. You can leave as many messages as you like. But mostly it'll just ring. If you're really lucky, you'll get through to a switchboard, and you *might* be able to get an email address; however, you usually need to know the name of the buyer first.

The buyers are the elite. I would imagine that it is pretty much the same in any industry, but it is so hard to get a buyer's attention. Most buyers in large retailers are bombarded every single day, with hundreds of new products or product ideas. It is really hard to stand out, and it requires persistence, and lots of time and patience raising your product and brand profile as much as you possibly can.

I can only speak from our experience with Gummee, of course. After a couple of years of not being able to reach an agreement with various UK distributors, we realised that it would be better to put all of our efforts into growing our brand, and the demand for the product, than desperately trying to find people that might agree to do it for us. This strategy may not have worked so well had it not been for social media, and the unbelievable opportunities that the internet has provided us with. The digital world and e-commerce have been our stable base, and home, for our beautiful Gummee business beginnings.

Throughout the rest of 2012 and most of 2013, we continued working hard at raising our business profile online. We entered lots of different awards, sent out lots of samples to bloggers and ran competitions on Facebook.

We couldn't afford to pay for any professional photo's or videos yet either, so we were making the most of the photos we were being sent by friends and customers, of their babies using a Gummee glove. Back then, amateur videos or non-professional videos were not really used for commercial purposes. Everyone was still getting to grips with social media, so the realisation of just how big it was going to be for businesses, was still not realised. With that in mind, I'd been trying to put together my own demonstration video for Gummee glove, but failed rather miserably. Mostly due to confidence and a belief that if it wasn't perfect, and professionally polished, we would not be taken seriously.

Facebook is amazing for a number of reasons, one being that it is a really handy way for me to keep a record of things that have happened throughout the Gummee journey. Here's an excerpt from my personal Facebook page that perfectly describes one of my attempts at a demo video:

'Trying to record a video of me talking about Gummee Glove for YouTube. God, it's hard!! I've developed a stutter, a twitch & a belief that two million people are hiding in my living room watching me making a complete prick of myself.'

HAND TO MOUTH

Chapter 7: Barb wire clad Porcupine's, voodoo dolls, and Twunts

Anyone who works with me closely or knows me well will know that sometimes, I completely let go of professionalism. Those times are not (publicly) often, and never when it could damage our business or reputation. They mainly tend to be the sort of times when someone takes my product and then claims that they are the original inventor.

I am very much attached, emotionally, to my business, my products, and my brand. I realise it isn't ideal to always be so emotionally attached, but sometimes the emotion gets behind the wheel in the part of my brain where common sense is supposed to reign, and it dropkicks it right out of my ear holes. The result is usually something that my solicitor wants to smack my wrists for.

In early May 2013, I received a message from a lady that I was friends with on Facebook. We'd known each other for around fifteen years, and she'd moved away to Australia. We were not close friends, but I had socialised with her in local

HAND TO MOUTH

pubs, with mutual friends. She was contacting me to congratulate me on the Gummee glove and what a fab product it was. We got talking, and eventually, I agreed that she could distribute Gummee glove in Australia. Funnily enough, she had been running her own jewellery business on eBay too and had a baby, so I guess I saw some kind of 'mumtrepreneurial' synergy between us.

(Please note - professionalism will recommence in a page or two.)

I really struggled with what to call the lady I'm talking about, for the purpose of this book. I considered Twunt. However, that word amuses me, and so I didn't want it to lose that ability to make me laugh. So, I have settled on Poohy McPoohface.

So Poohy was doing an awesome job in Australia. I say awesome: I mean doing an awesome job on Facebook. Her sales were great; we were learning together and helping each other. The Facebook following over there was doing incredibly well as she'd copied our marketing methods over there, as instructed. In early 2015, she contacted me to say that for personal reasons, she could no longer work for Gummee glove. She wanted to quit and gave me five days' notice. Nothing had happened, everything was ticking along quite nicely.

HAND TO MOUTH

In 2014, our very first competitor came to market. They were based in Canada, and although the design of their mitt was different, they had exactly the same laundry bag/travel pouch and even called it the same thing. They were using similar terms/words that we were using back then, such as 'Hands-free for parents'. The wording of their packaging was similar. They had very similar descriptions for certain features, they had crinkly paper inside their mitt, just like our Gummee glove. I still remember the email I received from Gummee's Kate after this product was launched.

One of Kate's jobs every Monday is to audit the internet and report back anything she finds that we may find interesting, or need to act on. She'd sent me an email with all usual findings and there, sandwiched right in between two pieces of good news, was a link to another teething mitten she'd found the Facebook page for. I don't remember anything else from that email, only how devastated I was for the rest of that day. It had happened. My worst fear. My product had its first copy. I was gutted. It took quite a bit of counselling from my team, but I had to process the feelings and look at the positives. If someone was going to copy, they were going to copy a great product and idea. Who knows, could it be that two ladies had exactly the same idea, with some exact same features, just on different continents?

(Insert a slightly sceptic emoji here.)

Almost a year later, another copy hit the market, this time in the US. The creator of this product was claiming to be the original inventor of the teething mitten. I feel the fury even typing this right now, which is totally ridiculous. *None* of us is the original inventor of the teething mitten. Martha Ann Bryson was the first person in the history of the world, to create prior art. **Prior art** is any evidence that your invention is already known. She applied for a patent, and for some reason or another, never actually launched a product, and the patent was not granted, for reasons unknown.

The results of the worldwide patent and product search that we paid for in 2011 proved there was nothing on the market. In March 2012, while we were at the Falmouth show with the first Gummee glove samples, Lamaze launched a teething mitt, which was also being marketed as a finger puppet for Mum and/or Dad. I was gutted as they'd literally appeared on Amazon during the same week that we got our Gummee glove prototypes. I wasn't deterred, however, and knew that there was a need for one that was designed solely for the purpose of teething, with actual teethers on it. I wanted to add the report that we received from the innovation company here, in this book, for information purposes, but also I have to confess, I wanted to add it so that I could prove my story. After discussing it with my publisher, I decided not to as it would just take up a lot of room, and doesn't make for interesting reading. I will always keep it though, just in case. It's my middle finger, to anyone that claims to be the original inventor, even though I claimed to be the original inventor in the beginning. This feels like a sort of embarrassing confession but, I did, and have always chosen my words wisely. Jodine Boothby - inventor of the world's first *commercially* available Teething Mitten. Because, after receiving that patent and product search report, and knowing there was not a teething mitten on the market, anywhere in the entire world, it *was* official. When I received my samples, I was holding the world's first, physical teething Mitten in my hands.

Back to Poohy McPoohface. The very last Facebook message I'd received from her, was to ask me whether I knew about the aforementioned competitor products. I'd replied that I did know about them, and I guess that helped her to decide to do what she then did.

HAND TO MOUTH

When we lost Miss McPoohface as our distributor, we were in a panic, as we knew we needed to find another Australian distributor, to keep up the momentum of sales in Australia. We approached a few; their details were provided to us by the Department for International Trading, formally known as UK Trade and Investment. I was introduced to the largest distributor of baby products in Australia eventually, by a friend I'd made in the industry. (Thank you, Cara!)

Luckily, we were able to agree terms with this distributor, and they got going with Gummee glove pretty quickly after that. While all of this was going on, I was trying to find out from P McP what she intended to do with the website domain that she'd set up (www.gummeeglove.com.au) and also the social media that she'd set up, using the trademark that was owned by us.

She had signed an IP assignment with us, which meant that anything she created using our branding and trademark, ultimately belonged to Gummee Ltd. This meant that legally, we already owned the website domain and the social media pages, but P McP was trying to sell it all to us for $18k Australian Dollars. It goes without saying that this was infuriating. Do you know something? It doesn't matter what legal paperwork is signed if you don't have the funds to fight someone in court. I didn't care about the website domain; I already knew by that point that we would ultimately re-brand to Gummee, so the website domain meant nothing to me. I wanted the Facebook page back. I had originally been an admin on the page, but she'd removed me at some point.

After a long drawn out process, I obtained some posh, red wax stamped legal paperwork that I then had to send to the Facebook legal department to prove that I was the brand owner, and they then added me back as admin onto that page. Getting straight onto that page and removing Poohy as page owner was, and still is, one of the most satisfying moments of my life. My face ached from all the smiling that day.

Around July 2015, I received an email from someone in the industry, to let us know that P McCPF was about to launch a teething mitten. I was furious, but not surprised. The whole time, *the whole time*, from the very first day that she'd said she was going to stop distributing Gummee glove, I'd said to everyone around me that it didn't feel right. It didn't stack up. My gut is very intuitive; it knew that this was not going to be the end of our dealings with Poohy. We sent a legal letter, demanding to know this, that and the other. As I'd suspected she would, she completely ignored the letter.

Meanwhile, we were making rough estimations of the cost of taking her to court. Travel to Australia, legal discussions to find out whether the case would be subject to Australian law or UK law, then the ensuing battle over what rights had been infringed. In legal terms, the distribution agreement (that we'd failed to get her to sign) would have covered us and possibly the court would have favoured an outcome that would have been in the best interests of Gummee. Who were we kidding? We didn't have the cash for this. Or the emotional energy. Or the time.

I was so angry though. I'd been able to process the first two competitors much more easily. But this was personal. Looking at our Facebook accounts, we had over forty mutual friends. I knew that the damage to her, through a public Facebook post, just detailing all of the facts, would far outweigh any result that a court of law would get for me. So, on July 27th 2016, and at the risk of another wrist slap from my solicitor, (sorry Tom) I posted the following status update, for all to see, and I set it to 'Public' in my Facebook privacy settings:

HAND TO MOUTH

In 2013, I received a Facebook message from someone that is from the same area that I live. I knew her before she moved away, not really well, but we had the same friends & I drank with her a couple of times.

In her message, she told me how she'd bought a Gummee glove & it had worked brilliantly for her son. We got talking & we ended up taking her on as a distributor in the country she now lives. She did a great job and obviously learned a great deal about it all.....

Out of the blue, she suddenly said she didn't want to do it anymore. She gave us five days' notice. She was going to be homeschooling her kids instead.

That was early 2015. She then refused to hand over the Facebook page to us (that we already owned) & tried to sell that, & our website domain for her country, to us for $18k. I obviously refused, as I knew we already owned it. The domain name I didn't give a shit about because I knew what our long-term plans were & they didn't include that domain. But I wanted that Facebook page back.

I had to travel to Exeter to get a special kind of solicitor to identify me & sign a special certificate, that I could then send to the Facebook legal team so that they would then make me admin of the page that this so-called friend would not hand back over.

HAND TO MOUTH

It worked, & they did.

I went straight on there and booted her off. (Would love to have been a fly on the wall the day she realised what had happened, mwahahahaha.)

A little while ago, we found out she is bringing her own version of a teething mitten to market. So she lied about homeschooling, & not having time to work on GG anymore.

Bummer. So people actually DO do this sort of thing? And not the big companies that you expect to.....it's not just in stories & movies, people who you once considered a friend are actually capable of doing this.

Anyway, I've agonised emotionally over copycats far too much; it's not the fact there's going to be another copy product to contend with (oh please, none of them are contenders) it's the fact it's HER.

We have a lot of FB friends in common, so I'm sure she'll get to hear about this post. That's okay; it's not slanderous, it's all factual. Oh, & I've set it to 'Public'. How can you live with yourself, *removed name for obvious reasons*? What did I/we do? Don't you feel ashamed?

————— has copied the Cheeky Chompers bib, too. I knew she was planning to do that when she was working with us, & I asked her not to, so she said she wouldn't. She even promised

HAND TO MOUTH

(June 2014) that she'd never dream of copying my products.

What sort of person does this? Obviously, someone manipulative, with no honour. No ethics. Certainly not business ethics. No loyalty.

Untrustworthy. Dishonest. Sneaky. All the perfect traits to create the karma she's making for herself.

She obviously forgot she'd signed certain legal paperwork which means that Gummee Ltd owns any teething mitten she brings to market within five years of the end of our working relationship. (That would be 2019, you unethical, immoral twunt.)

I hope your greedy ass births the barbwire clad porcupine I keep wishing upon you.

I hope you just keep re-creating other people's products & stick with being unoriginal, boring and unimaginative.

All the time you drilled me for info and I didn't think for a moment that you were doing that to do what you're doing. You were doing it to LEARN so that you could just copy. Nice one. At least you're not still learning from me! Phew! So much more I didn't tell you. All you can do is copy now, anticipate/second guess what we're going to do next, then get it wrong. I know all of your weaknesses. You carry on serving up your own karma.

Good luck.

HAND TO MOUTH

I'm going to play with my voodoo doll.'

I left it there, overnight. I can't tell you my delight when, the next morning, I had a message from Miss McPoohFace, who had gone to the trouble of unblocking me. She wanted me to delete the status, otherwise, she'd sue me for defamation. I took a snapshot of the meaning of defamation from Google and sent it to her. Then I asked her what part of the status update was untrue. Apart from the bit about me playing with a voodoo doll, what part of it was untrue? And I definitely *did* want her to shit a barbwire clad porcupine. Obviously, my opinions of her being unethical are just my own opinion, and for the purpose of this book, I would just like to state that my opinion may not be fact. The status update I have just shared with you is a very emotive one. I feel embarrassed reading it, however, it is relevant to the story, and it is honest.

It is a very risky thing to have done, with major potential legal ramifications with regards to defamation and libel, and I in no way want to suggest that it's the ideal course of action for anyone. I'd worded the status incredibly carefully so that I couldn't be sued for defamation or libel, and I deleted the status the morning after posting it as underneath it all, it didn't 'feel' right to leave it there. Plus, airing your dirty laundry online, professional or otherwise, is never a very good plan.

I asked Poohy whether she had received our legal letter (she had because we have the electronic evidence from the courier), but she didn't reply. But I was ecstatic. All the awful, insulting and unpleasant comments on my status, from people she'd known for most of her life. Each one must've felt like another knife in the back. There was even a comment from someone that said she was a thicko in school. Ouch.

You know the bird's eye view you get of people falling back on to a bed, or trampoline, or massive pile of dried Autumnal leaves, in slow motion, and they have the most animated smile on their face? That was me, after getting her messages. For about a week, maybe more. No court result would EVER have got that for me. Even if we'd have had the best possible outcome after a court case, we'd still have been massively stung by the expense.

It was a total and complete catharsis, at its absolute best.

HAND TO MOUTH

Chapter 8: Dragons, Angels and a ring of fire.

About a month before we launched Gummee glove, early in 2012, I received an email from a guy from an innovation company. I cannot remember his name, but that isn't important. He wanted to know if there was any way that I could hold off the launch of my product as his clients, two Scottish ladies, had a similar idea for a product and wondered if there was any way that we could perhaps help each other somehow. It was too close to our intended launch date at the NEC, so I decided not to reply.

After we'd launched at the NEC and returned home, curiosity got the better of me. I decided to email him back, to see if I could get some more information about his client's product idea. He replied and said that as I'd gone ahead with my launch, they no longer felt they could pursue the idea of us working together. I felt a little nervous and worried that they would launch their own teething mitten, but all I could do was wait and see.

I had more important things on my mind at this point, like my growing bump, and wondering how the hell I was going to keep working after baby number two arrived if I didn't make sure that Gummee glove was a success. Those months of being pregnant, caring for little Jimmy who was only a year old, and trying to get my business off the ground as well as still working part-time at the local shop were absolutely shattering. I sat up almost every night, until the small hours, replying to emails from around the world, researching the world of babies and teething, marketing and learning all I could about strategies and how to market a product with little to no spend.

I was not expecting to love motherhood as much as I did. I mean, don't get me wrong, I am *normal*. I have those days where I wonder how long it is going to be before I can get some of the old me back again, and I hide in various parts of the house with tears streaming down my cheeks and shoving chocolate in my face. I go from those days to days where I know that *nothing* could make me feel as complete, and as happy as motherhood makes me.

When the children were newborn, and until they started sleeping through the night, the nights were my favourite time. Exhausting as it was getting up so many times every night, I relished it. It was always very clear, in my mind, that this period of their little lives would be over all too quickly.

I would set up the living room and kitchen with everything that I could possibly need throughout the night shift, and I'd go to bed feeling prepared. Maybe not always looking forward to disturbed sleep, but at least satisfied that I was ready for anything that the night (and baby bums and tums) might bring. When one of them woke, it was *our* time. Silent, peaceful nights, of soothing them back to sleep with whatever they needed, and then just holding them on my chest. It was as if some sort of magic energy transferred between them and me, while I was snuggling them. A healing, tranquil completeness.

I'd tried to breastfeed both of my babies but failed each time. I'm not sure whether it was anything to do with my breast implants, and probably never will know. The first time around, with Jimmy, I'd breastfed successfully (if you count being awake and crying, almost permanently, for two weeks, successful) before we decided enough was enough, we were giving him the bottle. I was expressing milk for him so that Steve could do night feeds and the amount of milk that I expressed was reducing every time I did it, while the indescribable pain was increasing. It took me two hours to express one ounce from both breasts on one particular evening, and that was when I'd had enough. We went to the bottle. Meanwhile, my boobs where enormous, they'd gone completely solid, were square shaped, and my armpits had started to swell, too. The agony was worse than the actual birth; I can put my hand on my heart and swear to that. It turned out I had mastitis in both breasts, plus some kind of blockage. My father-in-law had to take me to the out of hours doctor at 2am one morning because I was beside myself with pain. I was given strong painkillers, and some medication to help stop my milk from producing.

I felt relieved to be getting over the pain, but mostly sadness, guilt and failure. That incredible feeling of love and closeness you feel when you're breastfeeding. The feeling of the milk rushing in is a feeling I have always struggled to describe. There is nothing quite like it. For me, it was a feeling of intense pride, bonding, and excitement, combined with incredible thirst. It felt like magic. I was absolutely gutted to lose it. When I explained it all to friends who had successfully breastfed, they'd say things like: 'You should have had a lot more support'. I am not so sure it would have helped. If my breasts were simply not giving any output, how could a midwife or health professional have helped? I had a wonderful midwife, who sat with me for hours, suggesting alternative feeding positions, treatments and tips for ways to cool my breasts down or try to ease the intense, rock hard swelling of them both, and tips for encouraging the milk to come out. Nothing worked; it just got worse.

When Charlie was born, I just couldn't get her to latch. The birth had been pretty horrific, and I was out of my face on pethidine, which had been administered twenty minutes before she made her entrance into the world, so it started to kick in after she was placed in my arms. I can't remember how many times I rang the bell above my bed, or how many times a midwife came and helped me to get her to latch. It was countless. The same thing happened every time; the midwife would leave, and Charlie would come off the breast, and I couldn't get her back on. After eight hours of this, I'd had enough. I'm not sure how many new mums experience breastfeeding this way. Maybe I have extremely weak willpower, I'm not sure. However, I didn't feel supported. I could tell the midwives on the night shift were getting impatient with the pathetic Mum who couldn't get her baby to latch, and I just wanted my daughter fed and for us both to get some sleep. I was terrified that I was going to experience the same issues that I'd suffered when I'd tried to breastfeed Jimmy.

HAND TO MOUTH

I asked for something I could express into but was told to just massage my breasts and squeeze my nipples to help encourage the milk. I could only get a couple of drops out. Great. My wonderful breasts seemed to love making me feel inadequate.

From never having developed properly in the first place, to letting me down when it came to essential nourishment for my little ones. I felt like a fucking failure. I asked a midwife for a bottle of formula, and I'll never forget the look she gave me. Yes, thanks for your unhelpful glare, and lack of support and encouragement, however, I can see you are worked off your feet and perhaps slightly stressed. I am off my fucking face on pethidine, haven't slept for two days, my baby won't stop screaming, my tits don't want to help and my vagina still feels like a small rhino just barged its way out, leaving a constant ring of burning fire. *Give. Me. The. Fucking. Formula!* (I didn't say any of that, I just glared back, and stood firm.) I got the formula. And a happy baby. And some sleep.

I enjoyed working at the local shop. It was an easy and simple job, and what I liked the most was the fact that I pretty much worked alone, managing the whole shop. I got to know quite a few of the locals, and it was lovely passing the time chatting with them. I could sit whenever my pregnant ass needed to, and snack on Cadbury's fruit and nut chocolate bars, and Revels.

No one tells you this stuff when you start out with your own consumer product, but when you enter a new country with it, you need to make sure that you have Intellectual Property Rights there first, and also that your product meets their safety testing requirements. Both of these can run into the tens of thousands of pounds. We learned the hard way, unfortunately. After realising our mistake, we had to apply for our trademark and safety testing for Australia. All the money that was already coming in, we needed to save to put towards another production run to keep us going in the UK. The local newspapers covered our story, and how we were looking for investors to help us.

At the time, I pestered the owner of the newsagents where I worked to allow me to plaster the wall behind the till with the newspaper articles. Reluctantly, he gave in.

A bloke used to come into the shop all the time, mostly on my early shift. I remember him telling me about how he lived next to the river and how he was feeling good on this particular day as he'd jumped from his balcony into the river, to save a duckling.

One day, (one particularly hot, very heavily pregnant and sweaty day) this same guy came into the shop and was in the queue.

When he got to the till he motioned towards the article and said: "Have you found anyone yet?"
"Huh?" It took me a minute to understand what he meant.

"The article. Says you're looking for investors."
"Oh, I see! Sorry. Erm, no we haven't, we've decided to stop looking now, and take it slowly and hopefully we'll keep selling and just grow slowly."

"Well," he said, "I wouldn't be looking for investment. I'd just lend you the money, pound for pound."

More customers in the shop now, I'm not sure what to do with myself.
"Um, erm, heh?!!! Um..." (Customers waiting.)

Not knowing what to say, and feeling the other customers eyes on me, I asked for his name and number and wrote it down. I thought about it constantly, until the end of my shift.

HAND TO MOUTH

How could I know if this was genuine? I didn't know him, not really. I came home and said to Steve: "Sit down. Something bizarre happened today."

I explained the whole thing to Steve, AKA Gummee Daddee, and showed him the piece of paper with the guy's name on it. Hubs is from this area and knows, or knows of, most people around here. He didn't recognise this guy's name. He called his sister Jenny who also is from, and lives in the village. She didn't know his name either, but she made the great suggestion of Googling it.

We did just that. We couldn't believe what we found. There he was, headline news. I was going to use the term 'infamous' but then realised that was wrong. Someone would be infamous if they were well known for some bad quality or doing a bad deed. He was well-known in the press for something he didn't do. Something he'd been found not guilty of. *After* serving twenty-five years in prison. There is so much to his story. He'd been through absolute hell on earth.

And yet, there he was, in the newsagents, wanting to help a perfect stranger. He'd come out of a living nightmare, was treated in a way no human should ever be treated...the guy that jumps into a river to save a duckling that had fallen from its nest.

Understandably, he does have his struggles and demons. Anyone would, after what he went through.

I called him, and we invited him for tea. Such an interesting, lovely, funny, and very clever bloke. He helped us and loaned us the money we needed. Pound for pound. No interest, no investment. Just a genuinely nice guy, helping us out. He is indeed our business angel, but also I think, just an angel.

We attended his wedding in 2016. It was difficult holding back the tears; it was a very emotional day. It was obvious at that wedding that Paul was someone very special, and that he'd found someone very special too. I was captivated and transfixed by the various characters we met and the stories they shared of how they knew Paul and his new wife, Helen. Paul had helped us to change our lives, and here we were witnessing such a special event in his life. His visible happiness shone. From the massive letters of L O V E on the stage to the Alabama 3 Acoustic band playing in the evening, and Taf Thomas, lead singer of *The Ghost of Fishboy Tractor* in his amazing Goldfish suit. The amazing larger than life character in a top hat, Be Atwell, and the photographer, Christopher Sharpe, in an awesome tweed outfit complete with waistcoat and tweed flat cap, sitting on the stairs of the pew in the church, snapping away with his camera. It was a real eclectic mix of people. I felt boring in my simple purple dress; I sort of wish I'd worn something a bit more feathery, glittery, and interesting.

We were so chuffed for Paul. I hope people are inspired by him and what he has been through. We can get so stressed and caught up in silly, everyday little things that don't matter. In these very uncertain times and with all the hate going on in the world, we need more love and random kindness.

People like Paul Blackburn are a reminder that loving instead of hating is a choice we *can* all make. I promise always to pay it forward.

Knowing that Gummee glove was not patentable, we decided that the best course of action would be to get as big as we could, as quickly as we could, worldwide. I smirked just then, writing that. How naive of us to think we could achieve something like that, so soon.

We, at least, needed national coverage in the media, as soon as possible. I'd always been obsessed with Dragon's Den, and so decided to apply to go on the show. I was invited to go for an audition, which I was over the moon about. However, I couldn't go, what with Charlie being so young and going through a bit of a clingy phase, and Jimmy was also still just a toddler. I was allowed to submit a pre-recorded video audition, which was shot in our bedroom, by Sam. I was so unbelievably nervous, even just doing a pre-recorded video, in my own home, that I needed to drink a bottle of lager to calm my nerves. It didn't work very well, and that video makes me cringe every time I watch it. It's on YouTube.

After an agonising two months of waiting, I emailed the BBC team that I'd been in touch with, to find out whether my application had been successful. The girl I spoke to said that there were two teams, each responsible for finding potential candidates to go before the Dragons. Her team were pushing for my application, and the other team were pushing for a couple of Scottish ladies whose product was similar to mine. The feeling, upon hearing that, was, I imagine, akin to being punched in the throat.

I would imagine that being the fastest dog in a dog pound, but being tied to a post while all the other dogs go for the steak being dangled over the fence, is a pretty similar feeling. Not that I am comparing myself or the Scottish ladies to dogs. Maybe that's a poor metaphor, but it describes perfectly how I felt. I was gutted. I couldn't stop thinking about it; I couldn't eat or concentrate. I had to find out what the product was.

I called the BBC back and spoke to the girl that had been dealing with my application, and she said for me not to worry, the product was for teething babies, but it was not a mitten. Not long after that, I received an email to say that I'd not been successful in my application to appear on Dragon's Den. I was absolutely gutted, once again. The ladies from Cheeky Chompers, Amy and Julie, did make it on to the show, and their neckerchew shot to fame in the nursery world.

HAND TO MOUTH

Chapter 9: Psychiatric help, an important shiny car, and global domination.

Time went on, and Gummee glove was still doing very well with sales through Facebook. At this point, our Face of Gummee glove competition was going mad. Gummee's Sam was helping to look after our Facebook and Twitter and doing an awesome job of keeping up with it all.

I was getting into the swing of being Mum to two little ones, and regularly attending the local pre-school with them both. I found that part of motherhood quite hard. I have always been very shy, (the last five years have forced me to get over that quite a lot) to the point where I am a bit socially awkward, so I find it difficult forming new friendships and meeting new people. However, I forced myself to step out of my comfort zone for my babies. It's all about them, at the end of the day.

I'd experienced the anxiety that accompanied the depression back in 2008, but nothing could have prepared me for the anxiety that hit me when my two little ones came along.

HAND TO MOUTH

I feel ashamed to admit it, but I didn't ever want to leave them with anyone. Ever. Not even their Daddy, at times. How awful is that? I've never admitted that before, and have tears streaming down my cheeks just typing it. I had to go and see a counsellor about it at the time, so she was obviously the only one who knew how bad it had got. Whenever I was separated from my babies, my brain would constantly play out the most horrific, unimaginable scenarios of what could happen to them. Writing them out would make me seem like even more of a nutcase, so I will spare you, dear reader, however, I am convinced that this must happen to other Mothers, too.

When Jimmy was just a baby, and I'd had those awful experiences of watching him choke and have a seizure, I became obsessed. He had a breathing sensor underneath his mattress, a sound monitor next to his cot and a video monitor. Even with all of that, there were times when I would insist on sleeping in his room, positioning his cot right next to the spare bed that I was sleeping on. And I'd lie awake, watching him, too scared to go to sleep in case…….just in case. I'd silently weep, just playing out the horrible scenarios in my head.

I think as females, we have an internal danger sensor switch, and it lies dormant. When we become mothers, it comes on automatically. Mine had come on, and then some fucker had turned it up to the max, and eventually it was forced over the max line and it was broken. I saw potential danger in *everything*. It was utterly exhausting. I was constantly terrified and paranoid about my babies. Helicopter parent, yes. Yes, I was. I dangled down out of the helicopter, too. Always right next to them, always with one hand outstretched. Waiting to rescue them from anything and everything.

(It is currently Mother's Day, 2017, as I type this, and only yesterday I called and made an appointment to speak with a counsellor. It is happening again at the moment, and I am not sure why. Jimmy is six; Charlie is four. And BAM, the anxiety is back. I had a day at the Spa, as my Mother's Day gift, just two days ago. I lay face down on the bed in the treatment room, and could not relax. I could not relax, because I didn't have my stupid phone in my hands so that I could text my husband, to make sure that everything was okay at home.)

In July 2013, when Steve worked out that I could start getting a wage from Gummee glove, I was mostly ecstatic because I'd achieved my initial dream, which was to be able to work from home while my babies were babies. To be able to drop everything for my babies, without having to worry about the consequences with an employer. I would get to witness all of those 'firsts', and look after them when they were sick, or just needed a cuddle or some attention. I could now put them first, always.

My second biggest goal was just around the corner. Steve was not very happy at work and was coming home stressed quite a lot. When he'd first started experiencing stress at work, I had vowed to find a way for us both to work from home at some point. I promised him that I could feel, within my very bones, that I absolutely *was* going to get him out of that job. Steve had been at Tamarfoods for almost twenty years.

The following month, in August 2013, Steve was also able to leave that job and start work, alongside me, from home. It was the most amazing feeling, for both of us. We'd achieved what was, at the time, our ultimate goal. When we started out, with any of my crazy business ventures, the ultimate goal, and dream was for both of us to be able to work from home, putting our lives and that of our families first, whenever we wanted to.

Here's a status update from August 2013, the week after Steve had left:

HAND TO MOUTH

'We just drove past Tamarfoods.
Steve: 'I used to work there'.
(Followed by loud cackling laughter.)
Thinks it's starting to sink in hee hee.'

So on with our plan for world domination of our Gummee Glove. We needed to get to market, all over the world, *fast.* Be the first, be the original. We realised the next market we should target would be the United States. We'd sold a lot of gloves there, directly through our website, so it felt pretty urgent to hit that market first. I found myself Googling international nursery trade shows, and found that the world's largest nursery trade show was being held in Las Vegas in October of that year, 2013. It was advertised on the UKTI website, which was United Kingdom Trade and Investment, now known as DIT - department for international trade, a Government department.

I learned we might be eligible for a grant, to go towards funding the cost of exhibiting at the show in Vegas, so I applied immediately, with constant butterflies in my stomach just imagining the flight there. I found the idea of flying terrifying. The idea of being away from my babies, incomprehensible, yet here I was, applying for this crazy experience. It is safe to say, that sometimes, my drive to succeed, actually drives *me*.

Within a few days, I had a call from the local UKTI representative, and we made an appointment for him to visit us and find out more about us and our business. I will never forget the day that Trevor turned up. Standing at our kitchen window, I watched him pull in to our drive, wringing my fingers and hands with nerves. The outside of our home was nothing short of a tip. The lawn had not been mowed in a long time. The drive was thick with moss, everywhere was overgrown, there were piles of broken garden furniture, tools, manure sacks, rocks and broken buckets everywhere. Who has time for the garden when you have two little babies in the house, seriously? Even the sofa was lucky if I managed to remember to scrape baby sick off with a wipe.

I watched Trevor get out of his very shiny, very important looking car. Sorry, Trevor, I don't know what make of car it is or was. But it looked impressive. And important. And shiny. I kid you not, I watched Trevor look around, toward the house, up and down the drive, and then he rolled his eyes and gave a slight shake of his head. He looked like he was expecting to interview a couple of absolute nutcases. And I immediately felt a

HAND TO MOUTH

bit less confident. I mentally prepared myself for a big fat '*no*' from Trevor and the UKTI.

We all sat in the living room; we had Lucy with us too. We went through the whole story of how we started, and what our sales had been like so far. We were four months into our second year, and our turnover was at £79k already. The first year had been £39k in total. Once we'd completed all of the questions, Trevor happily informed us that we were entitled to every bit of help he could possibly offer. We were eligible for the grant they were offering. We were all so excited, and it was official; we were going to exhibit in Las Vegas, in the hopes of picking up a US distributor.

At this time, we had finished developing our second product, Gummee mitts, another world first. I'd had scratch mitts for both little Gummee's, and none of them had stayed on securely. It was frustrating, always losing one or both. Charlie scratched her chubby little cheeks quite a lot, so I decided there needed to be a predecessor to the Gummee glove. I designed STAY-ON mittens, that had a secure hook and loop closure around the wrist, with the added benefit of a silicone bump surface, to provide gentle stimulation to little gums, if baby felt the need to chew. We would launch them at the Vegas show.

HAND TO MOUTH

Chapter 10: Police checks, what happens in Vegas, and emotional intelligence.

Geez, August 2013, what a month! In July, my parents came to stay for a couple of weeks holiday, and to help out with the babies. By the way, although divorced for twenty-three years, they are now great companions, which is super lovely, and neither of them has a love interest. They have a lot in common, what with four children and sixteen grandchildren.

I invited my niece Abbie to come for a holiday too; she was thirteen at the time. Before I'd left Coventry, I'd spent a lot of time with her older sister Shannon, my first niece. Their parents are my older brother Brendan, and his former girlfriend. Their relationship wasn't very good and they had some difficult times. Abbie came to live with us a couple of months later. It was a bit of a shock, going from being a parent to babies, to a parent of a teenager, too. I suddenly felt old. I was suddenly hyper-aware of my fashion sense, the way I spoke, the influence I had to impose and the image I had to portray. Social services had to come and spend a lot of time with us, watching how we parented the little ones, asking us very personal (and at times, intrusive) questions, but obviously necessary and understandable.

Steve and I both had to have DBS police checks done, and they also had to interview our friends and family. This was quite a stressful, and again, an intrusive and invasive thing to go through. A) because I didn't want to fail and not be able to offer Abbie a home with us and B) my anxiety was still ever present, it was my default setting, and I was convinced they were going to observe that I wasn't a good enough Mum to my own little ones, let alone suitable enough to take legal guardianship of my niece.

Stupid anxiety.

Thankfully, after a lengthy process, we were granted official legal guardianship of Abbie. She has been a wonderful addition to our family and has made it feel complete.

The next month was spent preparing for our exhibition at the ABC Kids show in Las Vegas. We'd never exhibited at a trade show before, and we had no idea what our stand was going to look like. We ordered a couple of roll-up banners, and had a professional quality video produced, then organised everything onto a pallet, including stock and a TV and TV stand. To save travel costs, and time, we also packed our suitcases on to the pallet, even though we wouldn't be leaving until a couple of weeks after the pallet left us.

Looking back, I honestly have no idea how we piled so much into our lives. I have always had a debilitating fear of driving, and yet in September of 2013, we decided it was a good idea to put me through a crash course in driving. An intense week, of five hours each day, driving around the busy city of Plymouth.

Jesus, the more I type, the more pathetic I feel. I have unbelievable, uncontrollable anxiety, and ridiculous fear, over the most normal and unthreatening situations. How can I have the courage to develop, manufacture and launch a product, borrow huge amounts of money from people, with a risk that we might not make it, fly halfway around the world to sell it? Talk to the most intimidating business people I have ever met, be interviewed on regional TV, and in a National newspaper, and yet too fucking terrified to get behind the wheel of a car? It's ridiculous. But then, I've never minded using public transport.

I am not sure where the fear of driving comes from. I have never been in or witnessed a bad car accident. I think it is a fear that my brain will suddenly forget that I am actually driving, and I will slip into passenger mode, start admiring the view, then career off the road, causing a fatality. Anyhow, I passed my driving test. I still don't know how, and I remember starting the test thinking: 'Never in a million years. I am not going to pass. So I'm just going to drive, and concentrate on keeping my passenger alive.'

October 1st loomed. We were in the month that the Las Vegas show was going to be, and I was petrified. My parents were coming to stay to look after the little ones, and we'd worked out that we could ask Lucy to join us as Gummee employee number 3. It would mean that she could look after Gummee HQ while we were away, and could also help out with the little Gummee's, as they both loved and adored Auntie Lucy. We were over the moon when Lucy accepted, and I am sure she felt that way too if a little apprehensive. We all still felt apprehensive. It was around this time we also found out we'd been shortlisted for the Nursery Industry Best New Product Award, and that I was in the top fourteen Best Mumpreneurs in the UK on Twitter. The Nursery Industry Awards would be held at the end of the month and being the most prestigious and coveted award we could ever possibly hope to actually win; we felt it essential that we book our tickets. Lucy and I booked the hotel.

HAND TO MOUTH

In this same week, I nearly wee'd myself with excitement one morning while doing my usual checks on Amazon and eBay. This was a weekly exercise that I carried out religiously, to keep control of our brand, and anything concerning us or our products, within the public domain. On this particular morning, I discovered that Gummee glove was the second best-selling teether on Amazon UK. At the very beginning, when I first had the idea for a teething mitten, I researched teethers that were designed for babies that were too young to hold a teething toy. The only teether that was marketed for this purpose was Sophie the Giraffe. She was the world's bestselling teething toy, and my eyes had nearly popped out of my skull when I read that her annual turnover was $129,000,000 per year. Sophie steadfastly holds her position at number one on Amazon and eBay.

The day had come. Steve and I got ourselves ready; I checked, double checked, and triple checked that my Mum and Dad knew where everything was and knew all the routines. I was very tearful and kept telling myself this was for my babies. It was for their future, our future. Our bills, food, and lifestyle depended on it. Do you know what didn't help? Traveling on the 13th October. In 2013. From gate 13. We spent the night at a hotel in London before catching our flight.

HAND TO MOUTH

At the airport the next morning, I was so nervous. Nervous about the flight, anxious about my babies. I must have really got on my Mum's nerves, constantly texting to ask how everything was. The journey to Las Vegas was a gut-churning, terrifying experience. Not for any reason other than my wild, out of control, unreasonable anxiety. The flight was ten hours. I felt sick, and gripped the armrests with terror as we took off. I pinned my head to the headrest, and just glanced sideways out of the window every now and then. When we landed, I was flooded with relief, but also a strange sense of emptiness. My babies were so far away, and there was absolutely nothing I could do for them if something were to go wrong. I know how silly this is. I know how ridiculous it sounds, even as I type it. I hope my Mum and Dad are not offended when, or if, they ever read this book, and hopefully they won't take it personally. My Mum at least knew that my anxiety was off the charts at times. I know how safe my little ones are when they're with the people we trust the most; I really do. Anxiety is almost a feeling of a lack of control. I guess I am a control freak.

We took a limo from the airport to our hotel, the Westgate Las Vegas. If I were to have a bucket list, visiting Las Vegas had never been on it. So not only was I not looking forward to being away from my babies, I was convinced I'd be getting stupidly bored with all the gambling. Not that *we* would be gambling, but the idea of hanging around in casinos whenever we were not at the exhibition filled me with boredom before we'd even got there. My impression of Las Vegas could not have been more wrong. Everything was larger than life; it felt like we were on a massive movie set. Walking into our hotel was mind-blowing. I was completely in awe. It was so surreal. Almost everywhere you go, you will recognise something, from a movie you've seen, or an event that has been televised.

We got to our hotel just as the sun was rising on a new day in Vegas, and we were too shattered to go anywhere. I sat on the huge bed, really looking forward to relaxing. Only, my anxiety had other plans. My brain saw fit to throw stupid and unrealistic scenarios into my mind, convincing me that I should be at home, forming the usually invisible shield around my babies. They were absolutely fine, with my parents and Abbie, being cared for better than I could imagine. I called home and had a little tear, not daring to speak to the little ones in case they got upset when they heard me. Or in case I got upset, hearing them, which I knew I would.

HAND TO MOUTH

I busied myself, preparing my outfits for each day, and Googling the crap out of things like 'trade show etiquette', 'best business practices in the US', and 'how to get a buyer's attention'.

After a little rest, we went off in search of the exhibition centre so that we could start setting up our stand. Thankfully, it was in the next building. I say thankfully; I didn't realise that most of the buildings in Vegas are the size of a small village, so even though it was only next door, it was about a one-mile walk. We found our stand, and we were chuffed to see our pallet was there, waiting for us. We were exhibiting in the UK Pavilion, along with around eight other UK brands. Once we were set up, we went back to the hotel for a shower and then off to explore, even though I was hanging out of my actual arse with overwhelming tiredness. We visited the hotel restaurant and after stuffing burgers that were bigger than a small cow, we decided we needed to sleep.

The next day, I woke with a definite spring in my step. Outside, even though it was October, was beautiful sunshine and bright blue skies. I didn't dare let my step get too springy until I'd called home and made sure all was well. I woke up to adorable photos of Abbie with the little ones, and felt much better, having had some proper sleep. WE WERE IN VEGAS, MAN!

I literally skipped to the exhibition centre, scenarios of meeting the biggest retail buyers in the industry in Vegas, and them all lining up to take on Gummee glove. We were there with a clear plan to find a US distributor. This was our first experience of a trade show. We'd never been to a trade show, only a consumer show. Looking back, it was an incredible learning experience. I laugh when I think of how naive we were. We bowed down to anyone that even honoured us with a glance, inviting them straight into our little stand and going straight into our pitch.

Steve was amazing. My flabber-was-totally-gasted with him. He'd told me our new motto, while we were there, was: 'If they look, they're in!' And he meant it. If anyone looked at us, or even in our general direction, he would chuck out that line, hook 'em, and drag 'em in. Even the big sharks. He was a pro. I just stood, open-mouthed, updating my Facebook status about how awesome my hubby was doing.

Me on the other hand, I could not be as confident as my hubby. I tried, but it didn't feel natural at all. I hate being cold called. I hate being stopped in town by people with clipboards and pleading faces. I hate my personal space being invaded by a sales pitch. So I am unwilling to do that to other people. It is true that people buy from people, and my experiences so far had only confirmed that for me. Don't get me wrong; my husband didn't put people off. They, generally, would still come into us. My husband has a natural charm and a friendly aura. He is very smiley, jovial and down to earth. It only takes people a few seconds to realise that, and you can see them visibly relax and warm to him when they do. I totally adore that about my hubby.

By nature, my resting face looks like I'm wishing death upon you. If you're a potential buyer, I would rather wait until you notice my products at a show, watch you to see if you appear interested, then try to catch your eye. I'll smile, and if your body language and facial expressions tell me you want to know more, then I will be ready. It took so long to even get that far, though. I felt intimidated by everyone.

Buyers were like royalty to me, and short of getting on my knees and praying to their feet, I wasn't sure how else to be around them. Unfortunately, there are some buyers (otherwise known as serial sample collectors and glory hunters) that like to take advantage. They saunter past, with their buying badges hidden, so you cannot see their titles, or where they are from. They are dressed very smartly, they are dragging a case (full of samples), and they look down their noses at you. (Note - I have momentarily slipped back into unprofessional mode.) They will stand with their backs pointed at you, angled so that they are still within the confines of your stand, but angled so that they don't have to interact with you. This is very clear body language to me. And it means: 'Look at my back. Maybe you could kiss my arse, while you are looking at it. You know, because I am more important than you, and I don't respect your silly little business. I don't want to talk to you; I just want to see if your product interests me. If it does, I will demand some samples, and if you look a little hesitant after that, I will let you know that you could be missing out on the container load that I may order for my non-existent country, next month. I know that will be enough to fool you, and you'll be too intimidated to even ask for my business card which, incidentally, I don't carry because my assistant has them all (conveniently) and she is a few stands away. And when I have your samples, without having even asked anything further about your business, I will go on to the next stand and do the same. And the next one. And the next one.'

We went out on the first night of the show, down to the hotel bar. We sat at the bar, chatting to the

HAND TO MOUTH

barman. His name was Arturo. Steve was very generous with tipping him, convinced that he'd serve us much quicker whenever we needed a top up. I think Arturo was just a genuinely nice guy who enjoyed his job and wanted to serve, but the extra-large tips didn't hurt. He recommended we get tickets to the hotel's current event, Rock of Ages, during which Lou Gram and Tracii Guns, of rock group *LA Guns* and originally *Guns n Roses* would perform.

It turned out that the show had not long started, and Arturo called into the manager on his walkie-talkie and asked if it was too late for us to go in. A few minutes later, a security man appeared and escorted us into the show. I have never really been into rock music, but the atmosphere in this place was awesome. I couldn't stop myself from just singing at the top of my lungs (ok, shrieking) and even throwing in the odd headbang. I absolutely loved it. When we left, I queued up to get my photo taken with Lou Gram. Before this night, I'd had no idea who on earth he was, but I was so excited after the show, I really wanted a photo with him, to remember the night.

We headed back to the bar, on a high after such a fab show and ready to drink a skin full of Vegas cocktail specials. At each seat, there was a gambling screen, built into the actual bar. A couple was sitting on the other side of Steve, and while we were sat there, they won $5000. Steve was very excited for them and became engrossed in conversation with them. Because of how we were seated, I couldn't hear or see them, so I decided to go for a little wander. Earlier on, I had spotted some of the singers from the show we'd just been to and decided to head in the general direction I'd seen them go. To my surprise, they were just the other side of the bar. I got to them and then bottled it. I didn't know what to say, and I went to walk away.

All of a sudden, one of them shouted to me. "Hey, you're English, aren't you?" It was Tracii Gun. I asked how he knew I was English and he explained he'd heard my accent while I was talking to Lou Gram. His other half turned out to be English, too, and she was chatting with me all about how much she missed the UK. When they asked me why I was in Vegas, I explained all about Gummee glove and my little company. They were fascinated to hear about it, but it felt so surreal and completely ridiculous that they were so interested in me! It was a mind-blowing night. So surreal, but so much fun. And I was hammered.

The last day of the show came and went, and we left the exhibition with over one hundred leads.

HAND TO MOUTH

We sifted through them at the hotel and separated them into categories of: 1) Hot leads 2) Maybe's 3) Dodgy. I know this does not seem professional, but it's genuine and honest and it's necessary. And it's my business, and my gut has never let me down. Although, I may come back to that before the end of this book….

So after the sifting, we had sixty-three great leads. Around fifty of them distributors in new countries. We were ecstatic, and we felt the need to celebrate. I have always been terrified of loud bangs, and I had always hated bonfire night when I was little. They were generally spent with my hands on my ears, trying to block out the noise and crying in a corner. God knows why I agreed to a visit a shooting range in Las Vegas.

A big black SUV collected us from outside of our hotel and took us to Machine Guns Vegas. The place was fairly remote, which didn't do my imagination, and in turn, my anxiety, any favours. It was definitely a once-in-a-lifetime experience. I enjoyed the buzz of it, the thrill of the terror. Is that a thing? I wouldn't do it again. Or would I? I don't know. Maybe.

We had one day free, to cram in as much as we could. It was day six away from my babies, and I was missing them so much I felt completely lost, and I physically ached for them. I really tried to enjoy the day, but I became irritable and argumentative. I felt too guilty to enjoy myself. How dare I have a lovely time, being away from my babies. They must have been missing us, too. How totally helpless I felt, being an eleven-hour flight, and a three-hour drive away from them. When we got home, I walked into the living room, and when my babies noticed we were home, they ran to me, clambering up on to my lap, just looking at me and giggling. Charlie cupped my face in her little hands, and just smiled a big, beaming smile. Jimmy held on to me and just chortled, an excited little chortle. I couldn't stop my tears of happiness at being home. I hugged them and the tears just soaked my cheeks. My Dad said it was a picture he will never forget. He said he could see the love pouring out of me, and the bond between mummy and babies. Obviously, they had missed Daddy too, and Daddy had missed them. You might have noticed by now that I am somewhat emotional.

Writing this book has helped me to see just how emotional I am. I do a shit job of hiding it. I really do wear my heart on my sleeve. I am learning how to be more emotionally intelligent in business, however, when you're used to a lifetime of your emotions being the more dominant respondent to any situation, it is a hard, hard thing to change. It has forced me to look at the people around me and how they respond to similar situations, and thankfully, they all seem to have so much more control over their emotions than I do. I am surrounded by people I truly admire, and I hold them dear and close to me. Without them, I would not be where I am today.

HAND TO MOUTH

Chapter 11: See-through dresses, saliva floors and canapés at Downing Street.

As soon as we got back from Vegas, I had to pack a case ready to head to Kensington in London, with Lucy, for the Nursery Industry Awards 2013. I was tired after the trip to Vegas, and I was feeling guilty about leaving the babies again. I was starting to realise I hated this part of running a business. Traveling and being away from my babies and my home. This was *not* why I'd started a business; the idea was to be with my babies *more*, not to be away from them more. Still, I scoured my wardrobe for something half decent to wear. I wanted something classy, flattering. All of my clothes were size ten, and I was now a twelve, so it couldn't be too tight (Have I mentioned I'm an emotional eater, too?)

I chose a little black dress, with a high neckline that was lined with embellishments. This would be my outfit for the evening of the awards ceremony. Lucy drove, and we made our way there the morning of the awards evening. We found our hotel and settled in, relaxing before getting ready to attend the Nursery Industry Awards 2013.

HAND TO MOUTH

Off we strutted, along the streets of Kensington, looking for the Kensington Gardens Hotel, where the awards were being hosted. We arrived, handed our coats in and tried to mingle with vaguely familiar people from the industry. We were eventually seated at our tables. I was seated next to a lady who distributed a very well-known brand of baby products. I can't remember her name, but that can only be a good thing, considering how she made me feel. We chatted for a while, and I have no idea what I said during our conversation, but afterwards, she blatantly ignored me. I mean, she went as far as to offer wine and bread rolls to everyone else but Lucy and me.

Lucy is completely unfuckwithable, and is never ever paranoid or insecure. If she ever does feel that way, I have never witnessed it, and it never outwardly shows. I mean, over the last five years, I can tell now when Lucy needs a minute or a fag. Or both. This lady's behaviour had not offended Lucy at all really; she found it funny if anything. I, on the other hand, being the oversensitive, emotional twat that I am, was highly offended. To the point where it had knocked my confidence and I wanted to leave. This woman, whether she knew it or not, had triggered a massive attack of imposter syndrome within me.

HAND TO MOUTH

(Imposter syndrome: **Impostor syndrome** - also known as **impostor phenomenon** or **fraud syndrome** - is a concept describing high-achieving individuals who are marked by an inability to internalize their accomplishments and a persistent fear of being exposed as a "fraud".)

I suddenly felt totally unsure of myself, and anything I'd accomplished. I was convinced that I was not even articulate enough to be at this table, conversing with experienced industry experts and highly qualified individuals. It is ridiculous that just one lady could make me feel like that. She even positioned her chair so that she was completely facing away from me. Thankfully, we were also sharing our table with two men that Steve and I had met in Vegas, Mark and Phil.

They distributed a huge baby brand in the UK, and they'd chatted to us in Vegas and had looked at the possibility of distributing Gummee glove for us in the UK, too. We'd not been able to agree on a price, but we'd stayed in touch. They'd been so genuinely helpful and encouraging. Lucy had got chatting with a couple of people on the other side of her, and they were all cackling loudly. Where- ever Lucy is, there is always laughter. She has a talent for sniffing out fellow fun seekers, and they laugh like they're sharing a really dirty joke.

HAND TO MOUTH

It was time for the awards to be announced. The lady that had made me feel as significant as a flea fart was one of the first to win an award. Not long afterwards, she won another one. Everyone clapped loudly and supportively, graciously. It was time to announce the award winners for our category. I shuffled uncomfortably in my seat. My heart felt like it was going to burst out of my throat. I have no idea why, as I was convinced that we were not going to win. And then we won. Best New Product of the Nursery Industry. Lucy and I had to go up to collect our award. I remember Lucy screaming, but I don't remember what I did. I don't remember collecting the award, but when we got back to our table I was emotional (surprise surprise) and (cringe) crying again. With happiness and disbelief. Lady 'I'm too good for you' couldn't have been nicer after that.

That evening, we were invited to go out for a few drinks with the fun people at our table, to a pub over the road. I had started to get a massive headache, and just wasn't up for it really, but I felt I owed it to the business, a celebratory drink….or few. I don't know what possessed me, but I wore the most stupid heels, and they squashed my feet so much that I felt like my bones were fusing together. I have a vague recollection of walking back to the hotel with my shoes in my hands and complaining a lot about my feet, but still, we had a great night, and hey, we'd *won* the bloody Nursery Industry Awards Best New Product! I felt like I was floating for days afterwards.

About a week later, the official photos from the night were available online for us to go and look at. I sat down to scroll through them and could not believe my eyes. My dress was see-through! You can see the shape of my pants. How many people had noticed that night, while the luminous lights shone down on me on the stage? Why hadn't anyone said anything? The photo that shows it all will haunt me forever now.

Meanwhile, at Gummee HQ, AKA the Boothby residence, we'd been busy sorting out and decorating our very first office. Our home is a bungalow, fairly well raised on some rather random foundations. We are not sure what the reason ever was for how the foundations were laid. Maybe something to do with the land it is built upon.

Below our bungalow is a huge cellar, made up of six rooms, all very long and narrow. It was like a maze of dusty, dark dungeons, which over the last five years has undergone some transformation to become a very convenient storage area for us. Attached to the side of the cellar, and part way under our bungalow is a double garage, which has its own toilet and two other rooms which were not in use.

Before we made use of the downstairs space, every room in our bungalow was full of boxes and business-related articles and paperwork. Our desk was behind the living room door, and it was fairly stressful trying to work like that, to say the least. I hated having to try and be a business owner at the same time as being a Mum, but looking back, in the beginning, I did thrive on watching our little business grow so well and all while being able to stay at home with my babies.

However, deciding to renovate the cold and deserted basement of our home was the right move, and a very natural one. Not everyone has that kind of room to run a business from, at home. We were so excited; everything just seemed to fit together.

A few days after returning from the Nursery Industry awards, Lucy and I moved into our new office. We chose one of the rooms leading off the garage (obviously, because who wants to work in a dungeon?) and Steve set himself up in the corner of the garage. We officially had our own little premises to work from, and room to store all the stuff that was causing so much chaos and disruption to our family life upstairs. I could commute down the stairs to work, and I could run up the stairs if I could hear that my little ones needed me. On the days that I worked, Steve or Lucy would be upstairs with the little ones. Even though I was just down the stairs, I still felt bad leaving the children. I often wondered how the hell other mums did it when they had no choice but to leave their children at a nursery and go to work all day? It made me feel like a twat for feeling as bad as I did. I was in such an anxiety-ridden state that I still felt bad, even knowing that this was what I was working so hard to achieve. My babies would have to put up with me working away from them (albeit only down the stairs) because they would realise in the years to come what it all meant.

Here's a status update from around the same time, on a day when I just allowed myself to be 100% present with my babies for the whole day. You know those days, when washing or even choosing an outfit for yourself just seems too exhausting, and you've been up during the night constantly for like, years? And jogging bottoms, hubby's baggy t-shirt and a fluffy dressing gown is the *only* attire required.

3rd November 2013:
I've had the best day with my babies today.

HAND TO MOUTH

I didn't get dressed; I didn't wash.....I just spent the day with my babies.
We made a Wendy house. We played peekaboo in the Wendy house. We graffitied the Wendy house.
We watched a bit of Santa Claus but had to turn it off for Mr Maker...,
We had some of Daddy's choc choc.
We played hide & seek.
We played tickle chase.
I wiped up lots of snot.
I had a code brown. (That's a measurement of ten on a scale of one to ten on a messy nappy scale, normally a two-man clean-up operation, but I coped)
We played Thomas the Tank.
We had loads of fun.
Loved every minute of it xxxx

Being able to use my Facebook account to help me to remember the order of how and when events happened, and how I felt at those times, has been extremely useful, and a bit surreal.

In this same month, our business was chosen as one of one hundred small businesses in the UK to attend a reception at Downing Street, London, in celebration of Small Business Saturday. Only one person from our business could attend, so I would have to brave this trip on my own.

HAND TO MOUTH

The date was December 5th, and I set off at 5:30am to the local train station. Like a twat, I'd decided that heels were the best option. Bearing in mind, I had to walk down a dark country road, in pitch black. Downhill. I would normally have been too scared to do something like that, but I think the excitement was over-riding any fear. I must have been operating on adrenaline or something.

One of the things that I do love about travelling, is the travelling itself. Whether it's eight hours on a coach or five hours on a train, to me, it is uninterrupted 'me time'. I can listen to whatever I want, read whatever I want, eat or drink what and whenever the hell I want. I love travelling alone, or with someone that also appreciates quiet time to themselves. I don't mind the occasional chin wag, me and Lucy have some right laughs and deep conversations. But if I am to travel somewhere on my own, I relish it, and I plan for every possible scenario. My phone is fully charged, playlists are prepared, audiobooks are chosen, and my favourite couple of magazines and snacks stashed in my bag.

I look out of the window and go where-ever my mind takes me, usually inspired by my playlist. I can be raving with my best mates at a 90's style club, lying on the grass of a perfectly kept lawn,

HAND TO MOUTH

surrounded by loved ones in the summer, walking down the aisle at the wedding we never really had, or delivering a talk and inspiring thousands of budding entrepreneurs. It's funny how my imagination can paint these pictures, and yet, in reality, my brain is like: 'Pity you can't dance' (not that that ever stopped me) or; 'Why does anyone want to listen to you?'

I had never travelled to somewhere like London on my own before. It felt like an adventure, and I was relishing the chance to find my way around and figure everything out on my own. Gummee's Sam had put together some instructions for me, which were pretty idiot proof, so it was fairly easy to work out what I was doing as soon as I stepped off the train. I found my way to a pub where I had arranged to meet some of the other small business owners, and from there we were going to go over to Downing Street together.

I'd been using Maps on my iPhone to find my way to The Red Lion pub, opposite Downing Street. I remember feeling a little stressed because the arrow on the screen suddenly stopped moving, and I was stood in the middle of a busy London street just shaking my phone and cursing at it. And then I looked up. I was outside The Red Lion. Oh yes, and there was Downing Street, right over the road. The arrow has stopped, because you are here, you twat.

This was not me. It did not feel like me. Not only had I somehow managed to find the bottle to agree to travel to London on my own, but I'd also travelled around London underground alone, and now I was about to enter a pub on my own. And not just any pub. It was a posh one. In London. I took a big gulp and walked in.

We'd all agreed we'd be wearing badges, to help recognise each other. I had visions of me walking about like a weirdo, staring at stranger's chests until I found my group. I didn't have to worry. A group of nervous people who did not know each other seemed to stand out in the crowded pub, but I'd also seen a message on one of our shared Facebook groups to say that they were at the back, and that confirmed for me that I had found the other business owners. I ordered a half of cider, to help calm my nerves, and then went and introduced myself.

It was a really exciting, interesting and surreal day. We had all queued up and been security checked, then made our way into number 9, Downing Street. I still felt nervous, but excited too, and made an effort to chat with other people and do some networking. Canapes and drinks

HAND TO MOUTH

were served, and then there was a talk from George Osborne about Small Business Saturday and what it meant. We gathered outside afterwards for a group photo with George, and after it had been taken, he was mobbed by everyone, all wanting Osborne selfies.

With George Osborne, and the photobomber

I saw my opportunity and just went for it. He asked me what the product was, so I explained in as brief detail as possible, and then I pointed my phone at us for the shot. Whether he was still trying to understand the product or was getting a bit worried about how long the selfies with all these people were going to take, I'm not sure. He doesn't look overly happy in the photo, but I do! And so does the photo bomber.

Outside Number 10

HAND TO MOUTH

Chapter 12: China, Germany, USA

We'd also started planning a trip to our manufacturers in China, under insistence from our business coach from Oxford Innovation, Rachel Woods and Trevor, our UKTI (now DIT) representative. After experiencing the guilt of being away from our little ones while in Vegas, I didn't fancy the idea of travelling even further away to China, and definitely not for two weeks.

I was happy for Steve to take this trip instead, and take his brother, Christopher, along for company. Their actual experience could not have been more different from what we'd read on the internet. Their hotel was above standard, everywhere was clean and they were treated very well by our manufacturers.

They came home with some great photos of the people I had been emailing for the past few years. And tea. Steve came home with lots and lots of souvenir Chinese tea.

Getting Gummee glove into the major retailers was a big ambition, so we had to book a stand at the UK's only nursery trade show in Harrogate in

HAND TO MOUTH

March 2014, organised by the Baby Products Association. We didn't have any idea how our stand should look, and we had a very limited budget. Once again, Google became our research resource, and we scoured the internet for inspiration. We could not afford any of the setups that I liked. Surprise, surprise! We were given permission from accounts, AKA Gummee Daddee to order a couple of slat walls, with hooks. We were planning on hanging them up on the back panels of our stand. When we got there and set up the stand, we were convinced it looked great, but when I look back at the photos, I do cringe a little. It wasn't great. I guess when you start a business and decide to go head first for it, without being as prepared as having absolutely everything professionally polished, there have to be some sacrifices.

The show was very quiet for us, and our stand was right at the back of one of the halls, facing a wall. We didn't get to speak to any big retailers, but we did manage to recruit a few independent stockists, and I made the most of the networking; swapping business cards with other businesses.

As we'd gone completely all in on social media, we had an attractive offer for any other business in the industry - exposure to our followers through a weekly competition giveaway on our Facebook page. It worked like a dream.

In those early days when Facebook was yet to impose all the restrictions that they do now. If only I'd have known then what I know now! I would have put a lot more effort into growing our page for free while we still could.

I found out at the show that the ladies from Cheeky Chompers were also exhibiting, in a different hall. I wanted to go and speak to them but had no idea what I'd say. Eventually, I somehow found the courage and went to find them. Amy was on the stand, alone. I took a deep breath and walked up to her. I started introducing myself, and she just gave me the biggest, warmest smile. Julie appeared after a while, and we all stood talking about our entrepreneurial journeys so far, and our new business experiences. They explained how they'd found me, just before they were about to go into production with a teething mitten. Upon finding out about me and Gummee glove, they had decided to abandon their idea. They'd then had the idea for a neckerchief style bib with a teether attached, and the Cheeky Chompers Neckerchew was born. Before they'd finished telling me their story, I had tears streaming down my face. They did, too. It was an

HAND TO MOUTH

emotional, touching moment and I felt so humbled.

On the second evening of the Harrogate show, the BPA put on an industry award dinner and party. Jason Manford was the entertainment for the show, and Lucy and me were very excited when we realised our seats were right next to the stage. During his set, someone's phone started to ring. I realised it was Lucy's, and I wanted the ground to open up and swallow me. Lucy nonchalantly removed the phone from her bag and started texting someone. This amused Jason Manford, who then shouted at Lucy that he hoped it was her doctor. Lucy replied that it was her other half and that she was just telling him she thought Jason was 'alright'. Everyone fell about laughing.

After he left the show, I plucked up the courage (ok, the wine had given me the courage) to chase after him and get a selfie. By the time I'd got back to the table, he'd tweeted me to ask where his free Gummee glove was. I was gutted. Why hadn't I thought to take one with me to the dinner?

A couple of weeks later, Lucy and I wrote a Gummee glove parody, made up of various songs, and we made a video, re-enacting what had happened during Jason's show. We posted it on his timeline, but I don't think he saw it, or if he did, he didn't 'like' it. I don't blame him either; he probably wouldn't have had his ear defenders to hand.

Around this time, I'd entered Gummee glove into a competition run by the winner of 2012's *The Apprentice'* Tom Pellerau, and Jojomamanbebe. They'd set up a competition where parents/anyone with a product idea could enter their competition, and if the judges liked the product/idea, you'd make the shortlist, and then it was down to the public to vote for their favourite product. It was a landslide victory for Gummee glove! The prize was the incredible opportunity to get Gummee glove into all of jojomamanbebe stores, of which there were seventy-six throughout the UK.

It was our first significant high street retailer. We were ecstatic.

Our next trade show came around, and this time we were off to Germany in September 2014. Lucy and I headed off, Sam was doing the show with us too, but with her being based in the Netherlands, she was meeting us off the train. Unfortunately, on our train journey from the airport to the exhibition centre in Cologne, our train ran over someone on the track. We had to sit tight for three hours while waiting for the police and emergency services to do their work. The poor train driver was pretty shaken up, so there was also a wait for the replacement driver. Whoever had been hit on the track, had not survived. Somehow, arriving too late to set up our stand, paled in significance compared to what had just happened.

We made it just in time, and thankfully Sam had got there before us and had started setting up. I was so excited for this show. It was a huge show, and we'd heard lots of great things about it. As you may already have guessed, I was extremely sensitive back then to any remote hint of anyone copying my products. On three separate occasions, I had returned to our stand from a break or a walk around, to be told that a couple of brand managers from a huge baby brand had been on our stand, asking questions about our intellectual property. I was angry, and I'd heard so many stories about people's products being copied, that I was already paranoid, and very wary of anyone asking questions like the sort of questions they were asking.

I knew I had to confront them, and even the thought of it had me on the toilet. Irritable bowel syndrome has nothing on my body's ability to turn my bowels into a gut-churning, nerve-wracked pooplosion when faced with any kind of intimidating, confrontational situation. But I knew that if I didn't do it, I would have been kicking myself for weeks afterwards. I found their stand, and stormed onto it, asking to speak to the Managing Director. Man, was I shaking. My palms were wet with sweat, and when I'm that nervous, I scratch and pull at the skin around my thumbs, right next to my nail. What is that area called? No idea, but anyway, I glanced down and realised my thumb was bleeding. I could see I'd done it some damage and I remember thinking how I couldn't feel it, but it looked painful. I was glad it was my left hand. I shake hands with my right.

The Managing Director was not around, and the guy I'd approached introduced himself as the sales director. I asked him why his brand managers had been on my stand, asking questions about our intellectual property. He reassured me that it would just have been if they were interested in licensing the product. I felt a bit silly and over-reactive. But I was very pleased with myself for doing it. I came away still shaking, and needing a glass of wine.

We made lots of contacts at the show, did some great networking and came away with lots of leads. We were starting to learn not to get too excited though. Potential buyers, from all backgrounds and all walks of life, come on to the stand, ask all the right questions and say all the right things, making your ears dance and your brain buzz with the picture of all the future success that they paint for you. Then you get home, email them and never hear from them. We'd been warned a lot that serious buyers probably won't pay too much interest until they see that you've been around for a few years and that your brand has success somewhere in the world.

In January 2014, I received an email out of the blue, from a US distributor who we'd met at the ABC Kids Show that we'd exhibited at in Las Vegas. She distributed a product which is famous for sucking snot out of baby's noses when they are congested. The product was a huge success and was stocked by most high street and big box stores in the USA, as well as thousands of independent stockists and chemists. She'd been impressed with Gummee glove in Vegas and had been on the look-out for a teether to add to her range for the previous four years. She'd decided she'd like to distribute Gummee glove, but there would need to be changes to suit the US market.

We were ecstatic and readily agreed after seeing purchase orders from her stockists for her other product, that I'd asked to see. At last, we had someone to represent us in the USA. We had to make quite a lot of changes, not just to the product but also to our branding and the packaging. I had already started to realise that we needed an over-riding brand name for all of our products, present and future. We'd had lots of ideas for new products, and we couldn't call them all Gummee glove, obviously, but decided that shortening to Gummee would fit perfectly. There are a lot of baby bottle brands, and baby pacifier brands, and nappy brands, but nobody really owned teething in the nursery industry. And I was frequently annoyed at having to search for teething toys in the 'Feeding' category of any website! I couldn't understand why 'Teething' wasn't a category on its own; Teething is a big frigging deal, people! Like, jeez, the lack of sleep, the pain baby goes through, the dribble, the sloppy nappy's, it takes over your whole family's life! Hello?! It <u>needs</u> its own category.

Our US distributor introduced us to someone who then helped us with our re-brand. We changed the packaging and the product, however, it was a long drawn out process. We are a small company, and making such huge changes incurs lots of costs. We were finally ready to launch in America in July 2015.

HAND TO MOUTH

By this time, we'd had our first two copycat/competitor products appear. I was in the early days of trying to learn not to take it personally, all is fair in business as they say. It doesn't matter how many times 'they' say it though, when someone is copying absolutely everything you're doing, including your strap lines and text form your website, it does get extremely, teeth grittingly irritating. Well, you've read this far. You know how I feel about them. I realised that they could copy as much as they liked. They were not me. They were not Gummee. They could not tell the same story. They did not have the same story, brand values, originality or passion. It was time to start portraying our brand values, and putting out there just how much we cared about our customers, our products and our brand.

Chapter 13: Taming a dragon, stalking, and cake orgasms.

I was obsessed with watching *Dragon's Den* on BBC Two. Not right from the start, but when my first inkling of entrepreneurial spirit started to stir, it caught my attention. After applying to go on the show, I made it my mission to watch every single episode, from the very first one. I made notes of questions that the Dragons might ask me if I were to get through to be on the show. I made sure I knew the answers to any possible question. One of the Dragons, Theo Paphitis, had left the show and upon discovering the power of Twitter, had started a weekly competition called Small Business Sunday.

Small businesses have to tweet about their business, and Theo selects his six favourite businesses, then retweets them to his 500k + followers.

Sam had been tweeting the competition for a while, and in January 2015, we were lucky enough to be one of the businesses selected. Sam sent out a press release, and all the local newspapers printed it; we were all buzzing for a couple of weeks. As part of the prize, we were invited to an annual conference hosted every February in Birmingham, by Theo and the SBS team.

It is an amazing opportunity to network with other businesses, take part in workshops on the day, and listen to the inspiring speakers that take to the stage. There was a question time panel at the end, during which you can ask business related questions to a panel of high profile entrepreneurs.

I took my brother Peter with me to the first conference, which was in February 2016. It was inspiring listening to Holly Tucker, founder of Not On The High street.com, and Mike from The Really Useful Box company. I watched them on the stage, goosebumps creeping up my arms while I listened to their amazing stories of success. Theo was on the stage with them, of course.

I was star struck by Theo, but also by the very sort of people I aspired to be like. To be as successful as. I had questions I wanted to ask, but I was too nervous to put my hand up. Even the thought of it had my heart beating so loudly that I was convinced that everyone in my row, the row in front, and the row behind could hear it beating. I could feel it in my throat. I said to Peter that I would like to ask a question, but was too scared

HAND TO MOUTH

to put my hand up. He kept nudging me: 'Go on Sis, just put your hand up!'

I didn't. Chicken.

From mid-2015 to early 2016, we were mad busy, designing and developing three brand new products, to add to our range, as well as re-developing the Gummee scratch mitts. It was an unbelievably stressful time. We realised, far too late, what a stupid idea it had been, trying to get so many products done and ready for a trade show that we'd already placed advertising for.

When Jimmy was around eleven months old, and before we launched Gummee glove and Gummee mitts, Steve had the idea for our next innovation. We were rushing out the door to go somewhere, and Jimmy had been really unsettled on this particular day. He was very clingy and kept shoving his fist into his mouth. While dashing about the kitchen, grabbing everything you can think of for the bottomless, Mary Poppins-style change bag, I gave him a formula scoop to inspect and play with.

I always use to sit in the back of the car with my little ones when they were in baby car seats facing the back of the car. The idea of not being able to get to them and soothe them when travelling in the front of the car was too much. I would find that unbelievably stressful.

I'd got into the back, and we were a few minutes into the journey when we both realised Jimmy was quiet, but not because he'd fallen asleep. I realised he still had the formula scoop, but had managed to get it right to the back of his mouth and was chewing on it. Now, I know that these things are not intended for chewing on, and I did remove it right away (swapped it for a cheese rice cracker) but I showed the state of it to Steve.

'Why isn't there a teether out there that is specifically designed to reach that area of the mouth?'
If there was, we hadn't seen it. We agreed that if Gummee glove ever became enough of a success, we should design one. We'd call it Molar Mallet.

In 2015, we were ready to expand our range. Kate and I were designing Molar Mallet, and Kate had had the idea for a pack of links with attachable teethers, which we'd hoped would be a simple addition to our range.

Since we'd launched Gummee glove, we'd received messages and emails from parents and carers all over the world, asking if we could possibly make a larger sized glove, for children with additional needs. We'd often be sent photos of the damage that some of these poor children would make to their hands and fingers, and it was heartbreaking. Lucy and I often couldn't speak for a while after reading some of them, and we were desperate to help. We decided, very early on, that as soon as we could afford it, we would make a larger size glove for these children.

We were excited to show all of our new products at the next trade show, which would be in Harrogate in March 2016. The stand had been rebranded, we'd been to Ikea and picked out some funky furniture, and I just knew it would be a game changer for us; the grand unveiling of our new branding and product range. I was sure the buyers would love it as much as we did.

I'd been researching innovative ways to get a buyers attention (other than calling/emailing/stalking them on Linkedin every week). At the Harrogate show the year before, the lovely ladies from Netmums put on a presentation about some changes happening on their website and within their company. They had laid out a table full of fondant fancies all made by the famous bakery, Betties of Harrogate. I selected a little yellow one and took my seat. I got my mouth around my cake, sunk my teeth in, and was swept up into the most mouthgasmic dribble fest that I have ever experienced. I am so, so sorry to the Netmums ladies, but I can't remember what your talk was about. I know it was really impressive stuff, because of all of the clapping, and I think I did clap, I mean with my hands, but the only clapping that I was aware of was my tongue, clapping the roof of my mouth, demanding more cake. And there was a lot more cake left on that table. To my absolute delight, they gave a box of four cakes to everyone that left the room. I felt like I'd been given real, proper treasure. I can not emphasise enough just how much these pretty little innocent looking fondant 'get in my mouth right now you naughty little calorie burglar' fancies are. Total bucket list contender. You should add them to your bucket list. RIGHT NOW.

I remembered those cakes. A lot. All year. A cunning plan was starting to form. They surely had the potential to light up someone's day in a busy, dreary office.

Kate mentioned how her sister used to say that some suppliers would send biscuits to the buying office as a treat, and they always seemed to make an impression.

Right. I'd made up my mind. Gummee branded Fondant Fancies from Betty's of Harrogate, would be making their way to buyer's desks all over the UK.

HAND TO MOUTH

I'd already found out the names and addresses of all the buyers that I wanted to target. All I needed to do was sort out the sending of the fondant fancies. We decided that getting branded with our new logo would be a nice touch. I contacted Betty's, and they agreed to make some samples and send them to me. (Is it wrong that I was more excited about being sent free samples than I was about actually carrying out this ingenious marketing tactic?)

At some point, Kate had mentioned that buyers might not be allowed to accept bribes, in the way of gifts. I mulled over it for a bit, and then I had what I considered to be another stroke of genius. Inside each box of product samples that we send to the buyers, we would include a box of 4 Gummee branded fondant fancies, and a letter, which would include the following text:

Please enjoy these yummy Gummee Fondant Fancies!
Note: These cakes are not bribery.
They are part of our sales pitch.
Please take a cake, find a moment and a quiet place, and eat the cake.
The pleasure you experience is the pleasure that a Gummee Glove can provide for a parent.
Because happy, calm, quiet babies = happy, calm Parents who can EAT. CAKE. IN. PEACE.

HAND TO MOUTH

Needless to say, the samples that we received were once again, dribblingly good. The boxes were all sent out, two weeks before the next Harrogate baby fair trade show.

We'd set up our new stand at the Harrogate Baby Fair, 2016. It looked awesome. I don't dream very often, but late in 2015, I'd had a vision of the stand design pop into my head during a dream. The next day, I got the design out of my head and onto my computer screen as fast as I could. It wasn't exactly the vision I'd had, but it was close enough, considering the small budget we had. Thanks, Ikea.

We were so excited and proud to launch our rebrand in March 2016. We had a great position, opposite some escalators that buyers had no choice but to use, to get access to the halls up to the stairs behind us.

Buyers from Toys R Us, Argos and Mothercare all visited our stand and were very complimentary about our products. They all thanked us for the amazing cakes, and luckily for them, we had more on the stand for the show. Toys R Us and Argos both said that they wanted to take Gummee glove. However, we would need to have an appointed distributor. My heart sank a little bit. We'd always wanted to look after our own distribution, and we'd managed up until now. We were supplying Jojomamanbebe direct now and had been for around a year.

We'd spoken to most of the higher profile distributors in the UK over the previous few years but had never been able to come to any agreement. It would have meant giving over far too much of our brand, and company, to someone else. I'd always been very keen on representing and remaining passionate about our brand, and retaining a lot of control over our marketing.

HAND TO MOUTH

As I've mentioned, while in Vegas, Steve and I had met two men, Mark and Phil, from a UK distribution company, and they already distributed a large baby product brand in the UK. They'd offered to try and help us in the UK, but there just wasn't enough in the margin for them and for us.

At the Harrogate show, Mark stopped by the stand and seemed impressed with all we'd achieved. I explained how I'd spoken to the buyers from Toys R Us and Argos, and that they'd were keen, but we couldn't find a distributor. It had been three years since we'd spoken to Mark or Phil, and we agreed it might be sensible to revisit the possibility of them distributing Gummee glove for us.

A great addition to our stand was the sofa. When we sent out our invitations to meet us on the stand, we mentioned that we had cake and a sofa. It really worked. And after nine hours a day of walking, standing and smiling, the sofa was an absolute godsend. Our visitors thought so too.

Within a month of the show, we met with Mark and Phil, and we were able to make a deal. We were over the moon! Finally, it seemed like everything was starting to fall in to place. Patience is not my strong point. I'm good at painting a dream, or a bigger picture so to speak, but I do tend to want things yesterday.

HAND TO MOUTH

Chapter 14: Plastic willy's, Fibromyalgia and Frenemies.

September 2016 was fast approaching. I do ultimately enjoy our trips away to trade shows, and once I'm there working and too busy to anxiously conjure up horrific images of the sort of accidents that my babies could be having, I relax a little. However, in the build-up to the show, being away from them is all I can think about, and I always feel a bit down and become irritable and snappy. I find myself constantly apologising to my other half. He understands, and bless him; he is so patient with me.

Under all the anxiety, I was still looking forward to unveiling our new products at this show, to all the international buyers, and our existing distributors, too.

It has never been as intense as other years, but for some reason, the fear of flying was growing on me. A glass of wine had been fine the first year we went, and the previous year, I had taken strong painkillers just before the flight. I use strong painkillers occasionally as I have Fibromyalgia and if I have not been looking after myself properly or have had any kind of heavier than normal stress, I am likely to get a bout of the old Fibro. My mum has it too, but she suffers from it a lot more than I do.

As yet, there is still a lot of mystery surrounding Fibromyalgia, and what causes it. It is defined as a long-term condition that causes pain all over the body, as well as symptoms such as increased sensitivity to pain, fatigue, muscle stiffness, difficulty sleeping, problems with mental processes (known as fibro-fog), problems with memory and concentration, headaches and irritable bowel syndrome.

There are lots of other symptoms besides those I have listed, but they tend to be some of the main ones. Mine feels like an oversensitivity, in every one of my senses. I feel pain very easily, emotionally and physically. I am weird about smells and tastes, which then creates food aversions, such as the one I have for chewing gum. I hate it so much that I cannot even bring myself to breathe the same air as anyone that is chewing it. You don't even need to have it on show, or be eating it, for me to know that it is somewhere on your person. I can usually sniff it out.

Loud noises. I cannot tolerate the television being turned up very high, and if there is lots of noise at once, from different sources, I can feel my stress levels rise. My face scrunches up like a bulldog's bum hole, and it feels like my head is about to explode.

Taste. If I don't like the taste of something, it will have the same effect that I explained at seeing/hearing/smelling someone eating chewing gum. My throat wants to close over, and I have to get away from it. Certain medicines have this effect on me. My Mum used to have to wrestle me to the ground to get any medicine in me, and it would almost always come back up again.

My sense of smell is like a dog's. I can smell things that other people can't. Unless your brain can make you think you're smelling something that actually isn't there.

Recently, I kept complaining about a smell in our living room. Everyone insisted I was imagining it, but it was driving me crazy. I got on all fours on the ground, and crawled around, following my nose. Yep. Like a dog. I discovered it was the wicker basket that we'd been keeping logs in, for the fire. I chucked it outside, and I am now friends with our living room again.

Whenever I get a fibro flare up, which usually involves intense, unrelenting, widespread pain all over my body, I am always taken by surprise. I forget that I have it, or that I am prone to attacks of it. When an attack starts, I Google all my symptoms. I never get exactly the same set of symptoms at the same time; it always seems to be different.

The one thing that remains constant is how painful and sensitive my body seems to be. As in, if one of my little ones leans on my legs or arms (which little ones tend to do a lot) I will often cry out in pain. I try so hard to control it in front of them, and it saddens me that they feel they have to be so cautious around me. At least they get to climb all over their Dad though, bless him.

I went to the doctors and confessed to having taken painkillers the previous year, to help me cope with the flight. The doctor asked if they'd helped at all. I'd explained they had because I felt relaxed and very calm. The year before that, I pinned my head against the back of the seat and only glanced sideways out of the window now and then, just as I had on the way to Vegas in 2013. I think I grabbed Lucy's arm at one point. I may even have left fingernails in the sides of the armrests.

The doctor very kindly prescribed some Diazepam. I asked him what they would do to me, worried I'd be unable to put my stand up after landing. He said I just wouldn't care about the plane crashing, while I'm in it, in the air. Sounded good enough to me.

Lucy had been busy organising her wedding throughout 2016. The wedding was going to be a week after we got home from the Kind Und Jugend show in Germany. She hadn't planned a hen night or asked anyone else to, and I felt bad dragging her away for a trade show the week before her wedding. I wanted her to have something to enjoy while we were there. I covertly emailed all of the ladies that I knew in the industry, who were going to also be exhibiting at the show in the UK pavilion, and asked them if they minded being honorary hens on the night of the industry party. Thankfully, they were all more than happy to oblige.

Sooooo, how does one sneak some secret hen party stuff across to Germany, without Lucy knowing anything? The pallet with all of our stand stuff had already been collected and was on its way to Cologne. The only thing I could do was hide the bits and pieces for the hen party in my hand luggage. Great idea. Until airport security opened my bag, and about twenty penis straws tumbled out. Screw feeling embarrassed in front of security, I had to hide them quick before Lucy could see them.

The first day of the show went very well for us. We'd met with a lot of our current distributors, and most of them ordered our entire range. We were buzzing, and SO ready for networking drinks in the UK pavilion that evening. We stayed until late, networking with other brand owners in the industry and unwinding after the first day.

As previously explained, Gummee glove's first competitor product launched into the market in 2014. It was the worst thing that could have happened, at the time. I'd been warned of copies, and we'd spent a lot of time worrying about it, and when it happened, nothing could have been worse.

Since then, two more have launched. I have realised since, that it's not just about Gummee glove anymore. We are a brand now and no one can copy every single thing we do.

I had been wrestling with an inner need, a gut feeling, to talk to the lady that launched the first mitt, after Gummee glove. Out of all the teething mittens that have launched since Gummee glove, she seemed more genuine and had her own, original ideas with marketing.

HAND TO MOUTH

Knowing Munch Mitt would be at the trade show in Germany, I couldn't stop thinking about going to talk to her. I wondered if talking to her, would help me get over that emotional 'hump'. I felt pee'd off, with getting so emotional about copycats and competitors. After all, what is wrong with being a trendsetter?

I couldn't help, but think that if I met the human behind Munch Mitt, my emotions would be easier to compartmentalise.

My kids had over twenty teething toys each. I didn't care where they came from, or who made them. If my baby liked it, I liked it. I would buy more than one if I thought for one minute it would keep my babies happy for ANY extra time. Like, OMG sitting on the loo in peace for three minutes was like a mini 'me' break.

So I did it. Shaking with fear, I went to find her. We walked, and we talked, and we were women, being honest with each other. When we finished talking, we hugged. We walked away from each other, with wobbly chins & tears in our eyes. We didn't exchange trade secrets; we didn't talk in detail about our businesses.

I didn't tell anyone about it. Lucy and me went out that evening to the industry party. Dancing with other ladies from the UK pavilion, I saw Melissa, right behind us. I put my drink down and was considering going over, but when I looked again, she was gone.

A while later, still dancing, I looked up and saw her, coming towards the dance floor. We held each other's gaze for a few seconds, she came toward me and handed me a glass of champagne. We gave each other a heartfelt smile and carried on.

I should say at this point that before meeting her, I asked if she could prove that she had the idea for a teething mitt at the same time as me, which is what she'd always claimed. She sent me an email that she'd received in January 2012, (before I made my idea public anywhere) from a design company she was in contact with. Her idea? A teething mitten, called 'Gummy' glove. Imagine that? And yes, I could be cynical and wonder if she faked the email, but you get a gut feeling about someone, and my internal bullshit detector didn't go off when I was with her.

I held on to that glass of champagne, and every sip was savoured. That drink meant so much. It represented the (somewhat) maturing of my emotions in business. It represented my acceptance and understanding (somewhat) of others. It represented my love of BUSINESS and my appreciation of other female entrepreneurs.

She found Gummee Glove a few months into her business journey and had to rebrand after soul searching and wondering whether or not to carry on. She decided that, as we're on different continents, she should go for it. So she rebranded to Munch Mitt & carried on. We had our first babies just two months apart. Both of our babies chewed on their hands, inspiring us both to come up with a product for a baby's hands. Our second child were both called Charlie.

That same night, was the industry party, and also, show time. I'd secretly distributed plastic willy straws and sashes to all the honorary hens during the day, and we were all excited to surprise Lucy. I'd always been overly cautious about getting too close to other entrepreneurs/brand owners in the industry. For some reason I allowed my insecurities to get the better of me for a while, and I felt inferior to them. I was convinced that they were all highly educated, highly intelligent, qualified, and experienced. This particular show changed how I felt. I started to realise we were all experiencing the same, or very similar journeys, with our unique brands and products.

HAND TO MOUTH

Back to the night in question. We arrived at the venue and found our seats on a table that had been saved by Emma and Warren Newton of Innovative Baby Products. Sitting with them, were the owners of the Milk Monster brand. Lucy and I took a seat, and the room was starting to fill up. The honorary hens started to arrive, and as predicted, Lucy went out for a cigarette. Sashes and willy straws flew about, and we were all kitted out, ready for her return. I could tell Lucy had been suspecting that I was up to something, but she was good enough to let me carry on, without question.

Lucy came back in, and she did look surprised. I presented her with a sash and a little 'bride to be' top hat, and like the beautiful, dutiful wife to be that she was, she wore them that night with pride. With the industry party being made up of people from all walks and backgrounds and cultures and countries, there were a lot of inquisitive people surrounding us that night. They wanted to know why so many ladies from the UK pavilion were wearing sashes and drinking through small penis's. When they learned that it was all about the bride to be, they could not have been more accommodating. Lucy was treated like a celebrity, and we formed a large circle on the dance floor, taking it, in turn, one by one, to dance in the middle of the circle. It was an awesome night, and I have some lovely industry friends to thank, for helping to make it so memorable: Rifat Jan of Fill N Squeeze, Sara Keel of Baby Cup, Emma and Warren Newton of Innovative Baby Products, Jennifer Unsworth of Tidytots, Emily Goodall of Bundlebean, Victora Samuel of Milk Monster, Suzanne Stokes of Tum Tum, and Keira O'Mara, of Mama Designs. You ladies literally ROCK!

The trade shows we exhibit at every year have always been exciting; you never know who you're going to meet or what could happen.

Attending them is invaluable. You can't measure the success just by how many orders for your product you take. The networking you do with other companies that are exhibiting is just as important. You can plan collaborations with them, increasing both of your potential audiences.

You can walk the show and meet companies from other countries, learn what makes a product potentially more popular in their country; a simple colour difference for example.

You can get inspired for new product ideas. I don't mean copying someone else's product; I mean taking elements of certain products and then combining them to make something completely different and relative to your market. You can spot other products in use and see an opportunity for a product to go with that product, that isn't yet on the market.

I always feel inspired at the shows, and during quieter periods I will sit and sketch my idea's, and then save them for future use.

This show was significant for us. At previous shows, I've watched other companies in serious business meetings, in the lounge area of the U.K. pavilion and wondered, when will that be me? Sitting with serious distributors, who are just as serious and passionate about Gummee products as #teamgummee are?

This show, it *was* my turn. And I didn't feel like an inexperienced imposter. I felt knowledgeable, confident, genuine and assertive. I was buzzing so much; I barely needed coffee! When I say coffee, I mean bucket-sized caramel Macchiato.

HAND TO MOUTH

Chapter 15: Big retailers, hippy's, and a 90's chav.

We came back from the show, to the news that our new product Molar Mallet, which we'd launched in-store at Jojomamanbebe, had become a sellout success. We were over the moon. Another amazingly successful product. Our UK distributors had been in touch as well to let us know that Toys R Us now had our Gummee glove on their shelves in the five biggest stores in the UK. When taking on a new product, big retailers will usually place you in a select number of stores at first to see how well they sell. Argos had also agreed to take Gummee glove into their online store, too.

All the big things that we'd dreamt of from the beginning were finally starting to happen. It felt as if it was all just rolling into our laps but. of course, that wasn't the case.

Gummee Daddee and I had worked really, really bloody hard over the last five years. We were (are) exhausted most of the time, and when one of these bigger things happen, all we seem to have the energy to muster is a 'Yay!', and then we'll have a cup of tea and get back to it. I think more than anything, over and above the sense of achievement, is the relief we feel when another huge step is taken. It means that we have the freedom of working for ourselves that bit longer. It means we're closer to the time when the littlest starts 'big' school, and that will mean that we've been lucky enough to have achieved being able to put family first, before work, for the whole of their baby, toddler and preschool years.

In 2007, when my business ventures started, I promised my husband that one way or another, I was going to find a way for us both to work from home so that we could put family and having a life first. I am of the belief that if you have happy employees, then you have loyal, productive employees. Creating a restrictive, austere environment for employees to work in, breeds resentment and an unwillingness in them to do their best.

I have never understood overly strict managers or directors who seem to revel in talking down to employees, or treating them like they are inferior. In previous work, I found that treating everyone as your equal, with respect and manners, is the best way to get what you need from them. If someone asks me to do something and they ask me politely, I will do it without question or thought. If someone is rude, I'm far more unwilling to comply. If I have to do it anyway because they are senior in stature, I will do it, but I will be wearing my fuck off face (sorry, can't hide it) and I'll do the bare minimum. Maybe that is not the best way to go about things, maybe more emotional intelligence is needed in those situations. I'm still learning, but now that the tables are turned, and I'm directing, I understand it to be more important than ever to treat everyone with the utmost respect and politeness that I would expect myself.

Apart from unscrupulous copycats. But you knew that already.

Family and home life is everything, and it is important that we allow our team flexibility where family and home life is concerned. We have never deducted pay for time off sick, for instance. This is because our team are so loyal, they work ad hoc hours from home to make up any lost time, without us even needing to chase them up. We know they won't let us down at any time, and I firmly believe that it is because we understand that family and home life comes first, and our team appreciates that.

We also allow them plenty of space within their respective roles to create and come up with new ideas. This is so important; it allows them to grow in confidence and enables them to feel job satisfaction, a sense of purpose, and see their own achievements, and feel proud.

Happy team = loyal, productive team.

The rest of 2016 was awesome. Lucy got married to the love of her life; my younger brother Peter got married to a wonderful lady who I am proud to call my sister-in-law, and we spent lots of quality time with my family and close friends in Coventry.

At the start of 2017, I signed up for a subscription service, sort of like a diet programme. During the membership, you learn a lot about the over processed empty calories we tend to stuff our bodies with day in, day out, and we also learn a lot about REAL food. Somewhere inside me, is a belief that we should only really eat whatever food is provided by nature, and it should go through very little processing, to retain the naturally present vitamins and minerals, as much as possible.

There is a real earth loving, peace-seeking, clean eating wannabe, within me. I want to eat healthily, run along listening to the birdsong, through the dewy woods and delicate spider webs at silly o'clock in the morning.

HAND TO MOUTH

My 10pm self-promises my 6am self, almost every night, that we will go running and be washed, showered, dressed and serving breakfast with a smile by 7:30am. My 6am self, apologises to my 10pm self, and switches off the alarm, and goes back to sleep, promising 10pm self that we'll absolutely, definitely be in bed mega early tonight.

I also want to drive to the beach in my 4x4, and run along the beach with the kids and a dog, in the wind and rain, wearing wellies and feeling all breathless, and virtuously at one with nature and all that is god given and pure. But I hate the rain and the wind. I don't drive, I can't be arsed to look after a dog as well as small humans, and I don't own any wellies.

I want to grow my own veg and be an eco-warrior, but I don't have the time or the discipline. My inner hippy is drowned out by the lazy 90's, chocolate cake loving, smartphone obsessed, loud mouth chav that I really am. It's like I have a split personality.

Anyway, back to this subscription service. On signing up, you are asked to think about your 'Why?' reason for losing weight. Just off the top of my head, I wanted to lose weight and eat healthily so that I could de-age, and look twenty again. Surely that is why everyone does these things? But then I was asked to go a little deeper than that, and ask myself 'Why', seven times.

The answer to my seventh 'why' would be my real reason for wanting to use this subscription. When I got to the seventh why, I was shocked, but shouldn't have been.

1) Why do you want to do this?
A) To lose weight and feel healthier
2) Why?
So that I will feel more confident, and feel happier and healthier
3) Why?
A) I will be more productive, and work better and faster
4) Why?
A) So that I can achieve our goals and make my loved ones proud
5) Why?
A) Because if we achieve our goals, we'll be able to afford to build the home we want, with the granny annexe within the grounds and loads of spare rooms.
6) Why?
A) Because then my family can come and stay.
7) Why?
A) Because I miss them like crazy.

HAND TO MOUTH

So, there it is. Underneath it all, my ultimate end goal is to be living in a dream home of our own design, with plenty of space for the family to come and stay whenever they want to, and ultimately for my parents to retire to. Seventeen years I have been away from home, and I miss them so much it hurts. I pick up the phone a lot and bore them to death probably, but I think they do miss me, too. After spending so much time with them towards the end of 2016, I felt more like me again, and it was a nice reminder of why I still want to achieve so much.

Chapter 16: Hohoho, #gummeeteatime, and a verbally incontinent twat.

The run-up to Christmas 2016 had started. I am an absolute Christmas nut. I love Christmas. I remember as a kid, starting back at school in September and we'd come home during that first week back to school, to find that my Dad had already started putting up the Christmas decorations. We'd be full of excitement, and the Argos catalogue would come out, all of us circling what we'd like for Christmas. It's no wonder I start to feel a little festive around the end of August.

Facebook had not long launched live video streaming, and as it was becoming more and more obvious that people favoured watching a video over reading lots of text, I knew we had to take advantage somehow. However, there was the small matter of being terrified of being filmed, to get over.

Over the last few years, I'd been contacted a lot by other people with product ideas for the baby industry, all needing help and/or advice. I had also been contacting more experienced entrepreneurs, asking for help. I decided to set up a Facebook group for us as product/brand owners in the nursery industry. One of the ladies that had been added to the group was organising a Christmas Baby Bonanza Giveaway, and over twenty-five nursery brands each offered up a prize for one lucky winner. Every night, for twenty-five nights throughout December, another prize would be revealed to the public via all of our Facebook pages, which, collectively, would have the potential to reach a huge audience.

I saw the potential of furthering that reach if I could do product demonstrations for each product, each night. It would be a great way to work on getting over my nerves, and I liked the idea of taking advantage of the larger reach with live video. Plus it would be getting my face out there, and that was beneficial for helping to get my brand out and for giving me a platform from which to tell our brand story and educate people about our products.

I offered to do the videos for the rest of the group, and nearly everyone sent me one of their products to demonstrate on the live videos. No backing out now! The first few were nerve-wracking. I had done a couple of videos before the live demo's, but they were a little less nerve-wracking as I was only talking about Gummee products and I know those inside out. Demonstrating and talking about other people's products was a whole new ball game, and I had to make sure I'd done my research on each of the products before even thinking about doing a video on them.

What with all the copy products being launched, I was determined to elevate our brand and use myself, if necessary. We're not marketing experts, but we know social media, and we have an amazing following. I was willing to do almost anything to make our mark and keep our position within the market, and grow. If it meant using my face and doing live videos, public speaking or even writing a book (hello, hello), then that is exactly what I would do. And then the wild ideas…..

I contacted QVC and spoke with a lady about the possibility of me demoing my products on QVC. Unfortunately, they didn't have a 'home' for baby products, so they couldn't see where it might fit in. At least I tried. And I'll try again at some point.

I finished all of the videos. Some of them went really well, some of them didn't because the nerves got the better of me. After a while, I started to realise that live video wasn't supposed to be perfect and polished. By the end of the videos, I had got over the fear a bit more, but I was relieved that they were done. I'd learned quite a bit about being prepared beforehand, and having all the right tools close to hand, and set up properly.

A few of the NIP's (Nursery Industry Productpreneurs) said they'd had a few sales afterwards, so that was confirmation that it was working. I'd also bought a mannequin, which I thought would be very helpful for demonstrating products designed for Mum to wear. She's called Maude. Lucy was absolutely horrified and hated Maude. For fun, I started leaving her in unexpected places around the office and garage, such as at Lucy's desk or lurking in corners, like a creepy scene from a 1980's B movie. She even frightened the shit out of a couple of delivery men, and the postman, too.

I kept wracking my brains, trying to come up with a way that we could do regular live videos on our Facebook page. I felt we couldn't do a live demonstration every week of our products as it would get a bit boring, and if we did, we'd need something to talk about. I wondered whether we could interview someone every week, but then thought it might have been tough trying to find someone industry related, that would be interesting enough for our audience, every single week.

HAND TO MOUTH

We have trade magazines delivered every month, and I often sit down and flick through them to catch up on industry news. Recently, in one of them, the results of a study had been written about.

The study had been carried out by a nursery brand, and one of the questions in their study had asked parents what they would do with an extra ten minutes in the day if it were given to them as time just for them, to do with as they pleased. Over 40% responded that they would have, and drink a whole cup of tea. I liked how those results reflected what we had been trying to do with our marketing at the Harrogate International Nursery Fair, with the cake. Our products are loved so much by babies; we like to think that they give parents extra time for themselves, too. Hopefully for tea and cake, but even if it's just enough time for some basic hygiene or using the loo, it can feel like an accomplishment.

We decided to attach Gummee branded tea bags to every order made through our website, along with an invitation to join us every Wednesday afternoon at 2pm, for a live video, with laughs and general chat, with Lucy and me. At the end of every video, we'd give away a product, live. We still had all the products from the baby bonanza that we'd taken part in before Christmas, and I wasn't sure what to do with them, so I asked the NIP's if they minded me keeping them to add to our giveaway box. That way, they'd all get their product demoed and shown during the chat, and a link to their page or website posted on our page afterwards. They all agreed, thankfully. Including our range, we had almost enough products to be able to do a weekly live video every week, for a year.

We decided to call it #gummeeteatime. Eighty-plus viewers tuned in to our first video, and it was a great success. Lucy and I really enjoyed it, and the viewers interacted with us so much, asking questions and telling us about their day that we didn't need to worry about whether or not we'd run out of things to talk about. To our delight, viewers started asking about our products, and what would be suitable for their baby. It was a brilliant way for us to then demo and talk about our products, without feeling too pushy or salesy.

It's been almost six months, and we're still running #gummeeteatime. We have a lot of regular viewers, and most of them have bought Gummee products, not just for themselves but as gifts for their friend's babies.

At the beginning of December, I'd had an email from Theo Paphitis's #SBS team, asking if they could put my business forward for an interview with an online business website. Obviously, I was over the moon and agreed straight away. In one of my replies, I cheekily asked what sort of criteria I might need to meet, to be considered by Theo to be a guest speaker on the stage at an #SBS conference.

Before I knew it, I'd sent my talk over for the team to review, and was shocked when I was then invited by them to talk at #SBS 2017. I was so unbelievably excited, but also could not comprehend what I'd let myself in for. I'd done five or six talks, but my audience had never been more than around ninety people, and I'd been terrified enough just doing those. I knew what was driving me this time though. I wanted the world to know my story. I *want* the world to know the story. It's my ego; I know that. I don't know why I have this incessant need, to be recognised as the person who launched the world's first teething mitten, designed solely for babies to wear. Why do we get so pissed off when people copy us? Shouldn't it be flattering?

I guess when it is a commercial product, it is different. You take it personally when someone copies your product and then copies your marketing because it feels like they're also taking your customers, and therefore your income, and therefore threatening the growth of your business, and it makes the bigger picture seem further away.

Still, what better way to give my story that big push, than to stand on a stage and deliver it to over a thousand businesses, and for them to then tweet about it in their hundreds, and for the live stream of it to be shared so many times, too.

I couldn't eat for the four weeks leading up to the talk. Every time I thought about it, my heart skipped a beat, and butterflies were throwing their own Olympics in my stomach. I was constantly on the toilet. I lost over 8lbs. I couldn't decide whether I was more excited, or more nervous. I had to get the coach to Coventry from Plymouth. It's amazing how music can influence your feelings. I put together a playlist of all the sort of music that makes me feel happy and excited while imagining myself up on the stage, triumphant, having brought down the house.

I was staying at my Mum's for a few days, as Coventry is right next to Birmingham. Not long after I'd arrived, a gorgeous bouquet of flowers turned up, sent from all the lovely ladies in the NIP's group, as a show of support. I'd been sent a few other gifts and cards from other #SBS members, all wishing me luck, and I felt so incredibly lucky, overwhelmed, and humbled to have so much support. Theo's team were sending a car to pick us up the next morning, so I got everything ready and got to bed early.

The next morning, my alarm went off and I felt sick before I even opened my eyes. My hands were shaking when I got dressed, when I brushed my teeth, when I drank my coffee, even doing up my shoes. My chest shook with nerves every time I took a breath. My Dad turned up, looking really smart. I was so excited to be taking my Dad with me. I just knew I'd feel a bit more confident, knowing he would be in the audience, watching me. The car arrived, and off we went.

We arrived at the International Convention Centre in Birmingham, and I messaged the #SBS contact to let her know we'd arrived. She came to find us and took us up to a suite, where breakfast items and drinks had been prepared. I only wanted coffee; the nerves had killed my appetite completely. However I did force down some melon and a couple of grapes. A little later on, I was taken to meet Theo in a large office. As if I wasn't nervous enough already. Theo's PR Executive took me through the building to the office where Theo would be. I remember trying to answer her questions coherently on the way there, and I remember not hearing her very clearly because my heart was beating so loudly, I was convinced it had made its way up through my throat and was now making its way through my actual ears.

I walked into the office, glancing nervously around. The wall of the office was glass, looking out onto the inside of the rest of the building. As I walked in, Theo was putting on a jacket, with his back to the door, looking out of the window, and there were three or four other people in the room. He span around, and greeted me with a huge grin and a jolly 'How are you feeling?' I was so star struck, I couldn't say or think anything other than 'Fine, thanks', and grin back, like a big dickhead, with a very limited vocabulary. 'Have you eaten? How are you feeling?' He asked me again. 'Yeh, yeh I'm fine!' I said again. Verbally incontinent twat.

Izzy lead me and my Daddykins back down to the conference hall, Dad took his seat at the front and on the walk back to the hall, a hand tapped my shoulder. To my delight, it was my little sister, Teresa. I was so happy I could have cried. She took her seat next to my Dad, and I was taken backstage to get my mic fitted. I then went and sat with my Dad and sis, waiting for the moment I'd been shitting myself about for the last two months.

HAND TO MOUTH

While I sat waiting, I was mentally giving myself a good talking to: 'No one is going to boo you off the stage. And if they do, your Dad is here. He'll get 'em. You deserve to be up there; it's not going to be scary, you're just sharing what you know. And you don't need a wee. You don't need a wee. Fuck. I need a wee.'

I asked how long I had. Could I squeeze in a last minute comfort break? I was told I should have time. I ran off as fast as I could. As I sat down, I suddenly realised I was wearing the mic. Oh NOOOO!! As fast as I could, I prepared a splash mat, throwing lots of tissue down the toilet hoping that it would minimise the sound of me going. It worked, thankfully, although it turned out my mic was not active anyway. It still would have been just my luck, if it had been on, and I'd have just sat there, slashing away like a noisy old camel.

I set my phone up ready to go live on Facebook. The time came, and Theo started introducing me. My photo appeared on the massive screen behind him, and my entire being became the embodiment of my unbelievably fast, booming heartbeat. The whole of me was beating. My throat went dry, my legs were shaking, and my inner voice was suddenly completely speechless.

HAND TO MOUTH

Fuck. You have to do this now. And for god sake, don't do your wee wee dance up there. I passed my phone to my Dad and made my way to the stage.

My talk went amazingly well. Once I'd started, it flowed out. Mostly. There was still the odd time that I'd forgotten to go to the next slide, but I apologised each time and made a joke out of it. I had practised, so so much, over and over again. I memorised the order of every single slide, and each one told a part of the story, so it was pretty easy once I got going.

Afterwards, Theo hugged me on the stage and presented me with a beautiful bouquet of flowers. Once again, I was speechless but elated. Floating on air. I was shaking but with pure adrenaline this time. I sat down next to my Dad, and he told me how proud he was of me. He said his chest puffed right out, and he kept thinking 'That's my daughter up there, that's my Jodie!' My sister hugged me too and said how proud she was of me. My phone was going crazy, with hundreds of text messages, tweets and Facebook notifications. My Dad needed to go and call my Mum to let her know how it went, and my little sis asked me if I wanted something to eat. She shot off to grab me a sandwich, and I sat down to take a break, and to talk to each person that had queued, ready to ask me questions or just congratulate me.

It took me days to get through all the notifications and reply to everyone. I was so glad my Dad had live streamed the entire thing to my Facebook page. It was wonderful being able to share the entire story with so many people, and reading so many positive comments, and feedback was so humbling. Most people said they'd had a little tear but were mostly hugely inspired. I was so happy. I'd been able to stand on that stage and share my story with so many people, and it jump-started my mission of getting out there and getting my story and brand heard and shared.

The opportunity to do the #SBS talk was invaluable. I will forever be grateful to Theo Paphitis for allowing me to do that. I watched him on *Dragon s Den* for years, we applied for his weekly competition and were selected by him as one of his weekly winners. I could then attend his annual conference and network with the amazing network of entrepreneurs and business owners that he had created. Studying and following other entrepreneurs that I admire and aspire to be like, has been extremely important.

HAND TO MOUTH

If you study their stories and listen to their interviews, you're learning for FREE, from someone who knows what they are talking about. They have been there and got the t-shirt. They are wise, and there are reasons they are as successful as they are.

Something that I really believe in is karma. I believe that to some extent, you receive exactly what you give out. I hate confrontation, or any ill feeling, or negative situations. Those things drain me and suck out my energy and motivation. The more I give out love, honesty and help, the more I get back. It sounds a bit cheesy, but it is true. It's true because it is yet to prove me wrong. Even if it involves me risking hurting myself in some way, I will help someone else, because it feels like I'm building brownie points for myself, and, it feels good to be nice. The next good thing to come my way I will thank the universe for, because it is usually what I was working towards, and so I'll feel like it is deserved. Maybe it is all down to attitude, and how we read our own situations and events. Maybe you're reading this and thinking: 'She is talking out of her bumhole now.' And you'd be perfectly within your right to think it. But it is how I (try) to live my life now, and it makes me happy. Gratitude is so important, and I used it to help me recover from

HAND TO MOUTH

depression. I will always endeavour to be as helpful as I can be to anyone that I am able to help, always. A way of paying forward the help that we have received from others.

Time is my new currency, and my loved ones are the most valuable things in my life. If Gummee went into liquidation tomorrow, the value I have gained in personal growth and confidence, and the last few years that we have been able to spend with our children throughout their babyhood, toddlerhood, and preschool years, plus the lessons we have learned, are all still there, unchanged, and invaluable.

The journey of parenting babies and a new business has been an exciting and intensely stressful roller coaster so far. We've loved every minute of it (apart from copycats. Oh come on, it wouldn't be right not squeezing that last one in!) Starting a business off the back of an original idea, or new product is exactly like having a baby. There was no instruction booklet about how to do it. We were not qualified. Your guts, intuition and common sense lead you in the beginning, until your baby or your business customers can finally talk and tell you what they need or want.

At this moment in time, Argos keep selling out of Gummee glove; Toys R Us are taking our entire range into sixty stores across the UK and placing us on the end of aisle displays. Sales in Mothercare in Ireland are going extremely well, and we're going in-store with Kiddicare.

We launched Happy Hands in March this year, our larger version of Gummee glove, to help children with additional needs such as Rett syndrome, Down Syndrome, Autism, global developmental delay and a whole host of other conditions. It has been extremely emotional seeing our products help so many children who desperately needed a product that helps prevent them from damaging the skin on their fingers and hands.

We're gearing up to launch another World First product in 2018, and we have enough new product ideas to keep us going for years to come.

I am so excited to see what the next few years bring, and also, jaw-grindingly impatient to be as big as I know we have the potential to be. We are the most amazingly supportive team at Gummee. Lucy came into work today with Gummee branded painted nails, so I think that says a lot about how she feels about our brand.

We're a family at Gummee. When you buy our products, follow our brand, share our content, or support us in any way, you are considered part of the family. Thank you, for reading this (if you have made it this far) and please, come and say 'hi' to Gummee's Lucy and me, over on Facebook @gummeeuk on a Wednesday, at 2pm. We'd love to hear from you.

HAND TO MOUTH

HAND TO MOUTH